Business Administration

The progress of several businesses was severely challenged through the advent of the COVD-19 pandemic, with several businesses collapsing globally. Apart from the pandemic, the business posture and dynamics of yesteryear have significantly changed, as the way business is conducted today, especially in this era of Industry 4.0 and the proliferation of technology-assisted processes, has created a new environment for doing business. Comparatively, yesterday's business seemed to have been in the "dark," keeping itself within limited geographical locations, contacts, and markets. However, business today, with the technological boom, has created a global village with the advent of the World Wide Web and social media that is redefining the way business is conducted especially in product and service development, marketing and publicity, customer attraction and retention, scouting and recruitment, and so on.

This book responds to contemporary calls for new ways of managing businesses with practitioner-oriented discourses on topical issues like business environments and how modern businesses can thrive in the same. It discusses in some detail the general composition of business environments, specific factors that influence the operations and decisions of a business within its environment, the level of control businesses have over the factors that operate within the business environment, and the need for businesses to be proactive and to strategise in order to take advantage of the opportunities the business environment presents, all while minimising the negative effects some factors also present.

The book provides practical applications while not losing sight of the theoretical underpinnings. Case studies are provided to elucidate the theories learnt and provide practical application to real-life situations. Written in easy non-technical language, the book also has practice questions at the end, making it an easy instructional manual for business owners worldwide. It is also a brilliant text for introductory students of business administration and management and covers important business areas like types of business ownership and how to start a business.

Business Administration
An Introduction for Managers and Business Professionals

Kwame Adom
Robert Ebo Hinson
Enoch Opare Mintah
Theresa Obuobisa-Darko

A PRODUCTIVITY PRESS BOOK

First published 2024
by Routledge
605 Third Avenue, New York, NY 10158

and by Routledge
4 Park Square, Milton Park, Abingdon, Oxon, OX14 4RN

Routledge is an imprint of the Taylor & Francis Group, an informa business

ISBN: 9781032602950 (hbk)
ISBN: 9781032602943 (pbk)
ISBN: 9781003458524 (ebk)

DOI: 10.4324/9781003458524

Typeset in Garamond
by Deanta Global Publishing Services, Chennai, India

Contents

About The Authors

Kwame Adom

Professor Kwame Adom is Associate Professor at the Burman University in Canada. He has acted as Senior Lecturer at the Department of Marketing and Entrepreneurship at the University of Ghana Business School. He has several journal papers, book chapters, and books to his credit. His research specialisation is entrepreneurship, and he can be reached at kwameadom@burmanu.ca.

Robert E. Hinson

Professor Hinson is currently the Pro Vice-Chancellor at the Ghana Communication Technology University, Honorary Professor at the Durban University of Technology, and Visiting Professor at the Lincoln International Business School in the UK. He has 30 originally authored and edited books to his credit, and his book collection can be accessed at www.robertebohinsonbooks.com. He can be reached at rehinson@gctu.edu.gh.

Enoch Opare Mintah

Enoch Opare Mintah is Lecturer of Accounting and Governance at the University of Lincoln, UK, Associate Lecturer at Chongqing Technology and Business University, China and a doctorate student at Kingston University in the United Kingdom. He holds an MBA (University of Liverpool, UK), an MSc in Governance (University of Lincoln, UK) Cert., Hospitality and Tourism Management (Florida Atlantic University, USA), and a BA in English (KNUST, Ghana). His research interests revolve around Environmental, Social and Governance disclosures, sustainability reporting, corporate social responsibility, nonprofit leadership, and education. Enoch is a member of the British Accounting and Finance Association (BAFA), the European Accounting Association (EAA), and the Institute of Corporate Responsibility and Sustainability (ICRS-UK). He can be reached at emintah@lincoln.ac.uk.

Theresa Obuobisa-Darko

Theresa Obuobisa-Darko is an Associate Professor and holds a Doctor of Philosophy in public administration and policy management, a Master of Philosophy in public administration, and a Master of Business Administration (Human Resource Management option), all from the University of Ghana. She has over 30 years of teaching and research experience in the field of human resource management, organisational development, leadership, performance management and public administration and has authored several journal articles and book chapters in these areas. She can be reached at tobuobisa-darko@gctu.edu.gh.

Preface

This book, *Introduction to Business Administration*, has been written with students and practitioners in mind. The authors have several years' experience in teaching and business practice. The book covers salient topics in business in a comprehensive manner. Thus, the book is a one-stop shop for information which is scattered in many books and saves the reader from reading several voluminous books before gathering the same information.

The language is very simple to make it easy for non-technical people in the field of business to understand. Also, the book contains current references on the topics which the readers can refer to for further information.

The book provides practical applications while not losing sight of the theoretical underpinnings. Case studies have been provided to elucidate the theories learnt and provide practical application to real-life situations. The book is therefore suitable for academia and practitioners who manage their own businesses or those who want to start their own.

Business administration in the post-COVID-19 era will not be the same because the pandemic resulted in new ways of working. The authors have discussed how the issues of business administration will possibly be like in the post-COVID-19 era.

The first chapter of the book provides an introduction to business administration. Here, the business environment is explained in detail. The business environment may be internal, which deals with issues within the control of the business, or external, which deals with issues such as inflation, fiscal deficits, and exchange rate depreciation which are beyond the control of the business.

Chapter 2 continues with forms of business ownership. In this chapter, the various business forms such as sole proprietorship, partnership, limited liabilities companies, public corporations, and cooperatives are described and the advantages and disadvantages of each form of business organisation are discussed. People wishing to start their own businesses will therefore be able to decide on the form of business they want to enter based on their objectives, the legal form of the business under which they want to operate, and the capital at their disposal.

The third chapter deals with how to start a business. The chapter provides a comprehensive guide for practitioners to follow in establishing new businesses. Issues discussed in this chapter include all the anticipated problems in business and how to surmount them.

Chapter 4 continues with how to manage and expand a business. This chapter provides a guide to prevent the extinction of the business in the formative years, and when the business has withstood death, how to expand the business and manage the expansion. Planning, staffing, directing, organising, and controlling are some of the concepts thoroughly discussed. Also, the importance of policies and procedure manuals is discussed. Furthermore, the chapter treats forecasting, decision-making, and leadership style.

The fifth chapter is devoted to human resource management. All issues in HRM are dealt with. The chapter begins with the definition of HRM and continues with other concepts such as strategic HRM, goals of HRM, objectives of HR, HR architecture, HR system, HR activities, and HR function which include people resourcing, learning and development, performance and reward management, employee relationship management, employee well-being, nature of HR policies, and importance of human resource policies.

Chapter 6 covers production and operations management. Areas covered include the definition of production, production management, operating system, operations management, scope of production, and operations management. The chapter ends with the concept of automation and its role in modern business processes.

The seventh chapter deals with marketing and all marketing-related issues. Issues covered in the chapter include the definition of market, characteristics of market, and distinction between sales and marketing. Other concepts treated in the chapter are the marketing process, Porter's Five Forces model, functions of marketing management, the marketing environment, marketing planning, marketing research, market segmentation, the product life cycle, branding of the product, and brand equity.

Chapter 8, which is the final chapter, treats basic accounting and financial statement analysis. Other subtopics treated are the nature of accounting, bookkeeping, accounting terminologies, reasons for accounting, and finally accounting ratios.

This is a must have and a must read book because it summarises the basic issues in business administration in a concise form. It is a good source of material for learning and revision for students and a guide for practitioners.

Chapter 1

Business and Its External Environment

Learning Outcomes

By the end of this chapter, you will be able to:

- describe the general composition of the business environment.
- explain the specific factors that influence the operations and decisions of a business within its environment.
- describe the level of control businesses have over the factors that operate within the business environment.
- describe the interactions that occur within the business environment.
- explain the need for businesses to be proactive and to strategise in order to take advantage of the opportunities the business environment presents as while minimising the negative effects some factors also present.

Chapter Outline

- Introduction
- Defining Business Environment
- The 21st-Century Business Posture
- Types of Business Environment
- The Internal Environment

DOI: 10.4324/9781003458524-1

■ The External Environment
■ Conclusion and References
■ Case Study and Chapter Questions

1.1 Introduction

Undertaking an assessment of the business environment a firm chooses to operate in is critical for the purposes of understanding the market forces and dynamics that support or impede business growth and sustenance (Gupta, Guha & Krishnaswami, 2013). Businesses therefore consider the interplay of the competing and complementing interests of the internal and external factors and how these factors impact business strategy and management decision-making processes (Yiu et al., 2007). The internal factors which affect businesses include components such as the mission, objectives, value system, vision, governance structure, and brand equity, while the external factors comprise the micro- (customers, suppliers, competitors, publics, and marketing intermediaries) and macro-environmental (socio-economic, technological, political, natural, global, and legal) constituents (Niemelä, 2020; Mason & Harris, 2006). Internal factors as well as micro-environmental factors are controllable to an extent, whereas the external environment factors are not controllable (Guerras-Martín, Madhok & Montoro-Sánchez, 2014). The success of businesses primarily depends to a large extent on how well they are able to manage these factors to inure to their benefit.

1.2 Defining Business Environment

John Donne's famous poetic line "No man is an island entirely of itself; every man is a piece of the continent, a part of the main ..." has been adapted in the business circles in another popular coinage as "No Business Is an Island" (Håkansson & Snehota, 1989). Thus, no business operates in isolation and it fundamentally forms a part of an ecosystem. Every business has some form of association or relationship with other elements in the ecosystem it finds itself in. The aggregates of forces, conditions, and factors in an ecosystem that influence the existence, growth, and sustenance of a business are what define a business environment. By ecosystem, we mean all the various components in a space that can be exploited to support the achievement of a goal (Kandiah & Gossain, 1998; Yoon, Moon & Lee, 2022). When all these elements are brought together, they constitute the environment within which the business operates. Essentially, the business environment comprises the internal capabilities and resources possessed by an organisation exploited in the face of the external forces and conditions which impact the organisation's ability to make decisions or develop products and services (Banerjee, Farooq & Upadhyaya, 2018).

1.3 The 21st-Century Business Posture

The business posture and dynamics of yesteryear have significantly changed as the way business is conducted today, especially in this era of fourth industrial revolution (Industry 4.0), and the proliferation of technological-assisted mechanisms has created a new environment for doing business (Molinaro & Orzes, 2022; Kumar & Sharma, 2022). Comparatively, yesterday's businesses seemed to have been in the "dark," keeping themselves within limited geographical locations, contacts, and markets, but business today with the technological boom has created a global village with the advent of the World Wide Web and social media such as Twitter, WhatsApp, Instagram, and Facebook, redefining the way business is conducted, especially in product and service development, marketing and publicity, customer attraction and retention, scouting and recruitment, and so on (Vrontis et al., 2022; Kaur & Zafar, 2014). Businesses are now exposed more than ever in terms of trade, partnership, and publicity. Technological boom has changed the economic outlook and climate of today's businesses and reengineered global trade and business in a much effective and efficient way. Various algorithms exist online to determine the performance of one's business and customer profiles, which impact the determination of the tastes, preferences, and buying patterns of various customer segments (Abubakar Aliyu & Tasmin, 2012). Technology has also made it easier for businesses to predict market and customer trends. In terms of financial management, quite a number of free applications exist that help facilitate record keeping, cash flow, revenue, profit, financial performance calculations, and principally how businesses can efficiently manage their finances in the most basic way without requiring the services of professional financial accountants (Abad-Segura et al., 2020). As regulations and rules evolve in response to a need, so also technologies evolve to meet market needs both at the local and global levels while proving helpful in terms of compliance with regulations (Freij, 2020).

The impact of technology and digitalisation in almost every industry cannot be underestimated. In Ghana, for instance, regulatory bodies for businesses such as the Registrar General's Department, Social Security and National Insurance Trust, and Ghana Revenue Authority have digitalised their operational processes, which makes it easier and more appealing for businesses to meet their regulatory obligations and conduct business. Finding and recruiting the right people with the right skills, talent, and competencies are undoubtedly key to a sustainable business (Potočnik et al., 2021). In this regard, social media has made business operations less cumbersome by improving accessibility to potential candidates, including applying algorithms which link online profiles to job alerts. Placing an advert on social media will get a business more than enough suitable candidates to choose from. Unlike before, when doing business in the Ghanaian context was perceived to be the preserve of the uneducated but the gifted, the narrative has changed owing to the colossal change in the business dynamics and environment today, opening up to all who are ready to take the risk. The world has never been more interested in entrepreneurship and innovation both globally and locally than now as many who have formal jobs also run "side businesses" to augment their incomes coupled with those who resolve to be their own managers and decide to start businesses after completion of senior high school or their bachelor's degree.

In the area of customer relations and service delivery, customers, especially Generation Y and Z's, demand instant gratification amidst competing alternatives, causing the nature and delivery of customer service to change in a course aimed at meeting customers' expectations (Dean, 2004). Due to the liberal nature of technology, anything short of meeting customers' expectations will incur their displeasure, with some aggrieved ones taking it to social media to share their experiences and discontentments which may have a negative impact on the reputation, product, and services of the business (de Oliveira Santini et al., 2020). In view of this trend, it has become imperative for businesses to strive more to exceed the expectations of the customer by delivering an unforgettable customer experience, which may result in positive reviews for the business on its social media platforms. This goes a long way to help businesses keep their reputation intact and spend less on damage control (Kizgin et al., 2020).

With the new way of doing business powered and anchored on current technological advancements, change has become inevitable, but it is left to businesses to apply apt intelligence to know how to exploit these new developments to their advantage. Today's businesses can hardly hide in their little corner and do business the old way. In fact, electronic commerce (e-commerce) has not only disrupted retail business channels and supply chains, but the accessibility to both business-to-business and business-to-customer setups is said to have so far made sales close to USD5.7 billion globally with a projected increase to USD8.1 billion by 2026 (Statista, 2022). Indeed, online trade offers more options to consumers, compelling businesses to champion unique strategies to differentiate their offerings and offer better value to the customer. Hence, for businesses to enjoy a competitive advantage and business sustainability, there needs to be continuous commitment to creativity and innovation as evidenced in giant e-commerce companies like Amazon (Bernardo et al., 2021).

1.4 Types of Business Environment

The environment within which an organisation operates can be categorised into two distinct types. These are internal (or inward) and external (or outward) environments. Both possess internal and external factors or elements that form the environment which influences an organisation. Figure 1.1 is a diagrammatical representation of the types of environments.

Internal factors refer to elements that are usually within the control or reach of an organisation. Examples of internal factors include employees, culture, value system, and technology of an organisation. An organisation can modify all the factors that fall within its internal environment to fit its operations. Although an organisation has control over its internal factors, it should be noted that sometimes it may not have complete control over all the factors (França & Ferreira, 2016). For example, holding employees to high ethical standards and maintaining organisational culture most often than not are a contentious area in organisations. External factors, on the other hand, are beyond the control of an organisation. Examples of external factors include sociocultural factors, economic factors, government and legal factors, and demographic factors. The factors within the external environment can be classified into two: micro-environment and macro-environment (Sapovadia, 2015). The micro or operating environment factors have a direct

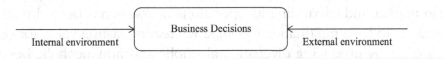

Figure 1.1 Factors influencing business decisions

influence on the organisation (e.g., suppliers and distributors), whereas the macro-environment factors influence the organisation on a broader level (e.g., political factors and economic factors).

1.4.1 The Internal Environment

Some essential internal factors that create the environment which influences the strategy and decisions of an organisation are value system, mission, objectives and vision, governance structure, internal power relationships, human resources, and company image and brand equity.

▪ Value System

The value system of the owners and those in charge of affairs of an organisation has an imperative impact on the activities of the business, especially its mission, objectives, vision, policies, and practices of the organisation (Bussmann & Niemeczek, 2019). A vital factor that plays a role in the success of an organisation is the degree to which the value system of the organisation becomes a shared responsibility by all the people within the organisation. A value system refers to an organisation's beliefs, moral aspirations and other value-producing activities it upholds and engages in, in its production and delivering of offerings. In selecting suppliers and distributors, an organisation takes into consideration its value system and the ethical standards among other factors.

▪ Mission, Objectives, and Vision

Business activities (strategy formulation and implementation, future direction, organisational policies or philosophy, etc.) of an organisation are shaped by its mission, objectives, and vision (Alegre et al., 2018). Mission is the overriding purpose of an organisation's existence; that is, it is "la raison d'étre" of an organisation. Business objectives are the defined, measurable outcomes a company hopes to achieve, while a vision is a futuristic picture of where an organisation would want to be and how it would want to look like For example, a Ghanaian company's, Kasapreko's, motive for entering into the foreign market and expanding its operations overseas has been driven by its mission "to be a multinational company creating lasting value for our stakeholders by producing diversified alcoholic and non-alcoholic beverages from herbal and other traditional blends using first-class technology" and its vision "to be the leading alcoholic and non-alcoholic beverage manufacturer in Ghana and beyond, satisfying consumers with excellent products through sound management practices and collective responsibility of all stakeholders."

▪ Governance Structure

The framework of corporate governance determines the allocation of rights and obligations among the various organisational participants and establishes the rules and procedures for decision-making (Shivdasani & Zenner, 2004). The governance structure of a business consists of the composition of the board of directors, management team, and workforce. Some organisational structure supports quick decision-making, while others are bureaucratic, which affects the flow of decision-making. The board of directors are the highest decision-making body of an organisation and are responsible for overseeing the performance of the organisation, and hence, the quality of the members of the board is a very important factor for the success of an organisation. In large companies or multinationals, the shareholding arrangements of an organisation could have important managerial implications on the overall governance framework. An organisation that has a lot of shareholders with voting rights may experience a dilution in management decision-making (DesJardine, Zhang & Shi, 2022).

▪ Internal Power Relationships

The nature of the relationship that exists among people working in an organisation determines the environment which can either promote or inhibit the success of an organisation (Herington, Johnson & Scott, 2006). If there is a strained or non-cordial relationship between employees and management, members of the board and the shareholders, executives and managers, it is obvious that decision implementation will be difficult as, for example, Herington et al. (2006) noted that successful client interactions are contingent upon effective internal relations.

▪ Human Resources

The human resources of an organisation play an important role in its growth. Features such as the skills, level of commitment, attitude, morale, and quality of the staff assist in defining the working atmosphere and environment of an organisation (Adero & Odiyo, 2020). Organisations that find it difficult to drive thriving employee relations within the organisations negatively impact the internal environment of the organisation. Employee relations in an organisation can differ from one to another as the culture of an organisation and its environment influence these factors.

■ Company Image and Brand Equity

Both the image of an organisation and its brand equity are critical keys that influence the internal environment of organisations (Zhang, 2015). Organisations must therefore do everything possible to build a positive brand image and equity. The benefits of developing brand image and equity help an organisation build a positive reputation and enhance their public appeal for partnerships with other firms (Brahmbhatt & Shah, 2017).

1.4.2 The External Environment

As mentioned before, the external environment may be categorised as the micro-environment and the macro-environment.

1.4.2.1 Micro-environment

A micro-environment is the direct and immediate external environment of an organisation. The micro-environment of an organisation is made up of players in its immediate environment that influences its operational activities and performance (Cabrera & Mauricio, 2017). It consists of competitors, suppliers, marketing intermediaries, customers, lenders, and creditors. Forces within the micro-environment directly affect an organisation but do not certainly have the same rippling effect in all organisations across several industries. For example, changes in a competitor's employee compensation strategy are likely to affect an organisation directly.

■ Suppliers

Suppliers or vendors of an organisation refer to the people or institutions that provide products and services to the organisation based on usual and strategic needs (Qudrat-Ullah & Szulanski, 2022). Hence, suppliers are crucial forces in the micro-environment of an organisation as the relevance of dependable sources of supply to the smooth operation of the business cannot be compromised. The unreliability on the part of some suppliers have forced many organisations into the practice of multiple sourcing except for highly technical and sophisticated products, which are kept for sole sourcing for patent and security purposes. Organisations also keep a high level of professionalism with their suppliers as a way of maintaining stability in the immediate external environment.

■ Customers

Customers refer to all persons or organisations (individuals, households, governments, and commercial establishments) who act as clients for an organisation and at whom products and services are directed or for whom they are produced (Wilkinson, Young & Freytag, 2005). Without customers, an organisation has no business and, hence, cannot exist. It is the responsibility of an organisation to attract and maintain customers. For example, the customers of Unilever can include individuals, distributors, wholesalers, and retailers,. The customer environment is gradually becoming global as an outcome of business globalisation, with local markets opening up to foreign customers and vice versa.

■ Competitors

Competitors of an organisation identify themselves as organisations that equally produce or deliver same or similar products and services, hence competing for customer share in an industry (Werle & Laumer, 2022). Competitors do not necessarily constitute those from the same industries but also other industries but within the same sector. For instance, the competition for an automobile company like Toyota may be Audi, as both are in the fossil fuel usage industry. A company like Tesla that is solely an electric car manufacturer may also be a competitor for fossil fuel car producers. Another competitor may be the scooter or electric bike manufacturers who are not into car manufacturing but into services that help people commute from one place to another. All these industries are competitors in the transportation industry competing for customers.

■ Marketing Intermediaries

An organisation's direct environment may comprise its direct intermediaries. An intermediary refers to "agents, institutions, merchants, etc., who assist an organisation in getting its products to the final consumers" (Virtanen et al., 2022). In other words, the role of an intermediary is to "help an organisation to promote, sell and distribute its goods and services to the final consumers." Marketing intermediaries play a very important role between organisations and final buyers of their products and services (Kannan, Chang & Whinston, 2000).

■ Investors

Investors, be it individual or institutional, of an organisation are simply all the people and institutions that invest their funds into an organisation in return for a dividend or an interest (Likoko & Kini, 2017). These investors also have a significant interest in the activities of the organisation to ensure that they invest responsibly and protect the social and environmental interest of the society. Apart from their financial investment, their engaged knowledge, connections, and capabilities give non-financial support to the organisation.

■ Publics

The range of persons with vested interest in an organisation constitutes its publics in the immediate external environment. These persons are termed as stakeholder; thus, a stakeholder is a party that has an interest in a business and can either influence or be influenced by it. These groups of people, depending on their interest in the activities run by the organisation, respond differently in varying degrees to organisational decision-making and outcomes (Nwanji & Howell, 2007).

1.4.2.2 Macro-environment

The macro-environment of an organisation is its largest and complex external environment. The forces within the macro-environment are uncontrollable and have significant influence on an organisation (Jiang et al., 2022). For example, the policies of a new government or the introduction of a new rule by regulators can significantly affect the operations of an organisation. Since the forces in this environment are uncontrollable, organisations in their bid to succeed must learn to adapt to these forces within the environment. One of the widely used models or frameworks in underscoring macro-environmental factors is the PESTEL analysis which breaks down as political, economic, social, technological, environment, and legal (e.g., see, Christodoulou & Cullinane, 2019).

▪ Political Environment

These establish the extent to which government and government policies may have an effect on a certain organisation or industry. This would encompass political policy and stability in addition to trade, fiscal, and taxing measures. The influence of the three political institutions (judiciary, executive, and legislature) can have a significant impact on an organisation's activities. An organisation will better thrive in a more steady and friendly political environment.

▪ Economic Environment

An economy's performance has a direct effect on the organisation's profitability. Included in the economic environmental outlook are interest rates, employment or unemployment rates, the cost of raw materials, inflation, and foreign currency rates.

▪ Social Environment

Emphasis is placed on the social environment and the identification of emerging trends. This enables an organisation to better comprehend consumer demands and desires in a social and cultural context. Changes in family demographics, education levels, cultural trends, attitudes, and lifestyles are some of the factors. An organisation operates in an environment that consists of all kinds of people with different cultures, beliefs, and societal value systems. The challenge here is for organisations to understand the different sociocultural context they operate in.

▪ Technological Environment

Technical considerations take into account the rate of technological innovation and development that could influence a market or sector. Changes in digital or mobile technologies, automation, research, and the quality of human resource and development could all have a role. There is often a temptation to focus solely on advancements in digital technology, but new methods of distribution, production, managing the human resource, and logistics must also be considered.

■ Natural Environment

Environmental factors are those that are impacted by the surrounding environment and ecological factors. With the increasing significance of corporate sustainability responsibility (CSR) and sustainability, this factor is becoming more fundamental to how businesses must operate. Climate, recycling techniques, carbon footprint, waste disposal, and sustainability are elements to consider.

■ Legal Environment

An organisation must understand what is legal and be allowed within the territories they operate in. They also must be aware of any change in legislation and the impact this may have on the business' operations. Factors include employment legislation, consumer law, health and safety, and international as well as trade regulation and restrictions.

1.4.3 Conclusion

The role of business environment is critical to the rise or fall of organisations. Specifically, this chapter focuses on the internal and external environments that shape the business orientation of organisations. The factors that define the internal and external business environment are discussed including examples of industry scenarios. Businesses thus explore both the internal and external environments for the benefit of their organisations. The macro-environment, however, presents mixed factors, some of which are partially controllable, with others being uncontrollable.

The onset of the COVID-19 pandemic resulted in a change in the internal operations of most businesses. In the midst of the Covid, there were lockdowns and most businesses adopted ways of reaching their staff and clients electronically. With a reduction of the intensity of the COVID-19 pandemic, these electronic means such as online trading, Zoom, Google Teams, Skype, among others have come to stay to facilitate business operation.

The external business environment was also affected by the COVID-19 pandemic, as most countries' macro-economic environment was impacted negatively, resulting in inflation, high unemployment rates, budget deficits, among others. Managers of economies are grappling with the problems of restoring their economies to be able to withstand such unexpected hazards.

References

Abad-Segura, E., González-Zamar, M.D., López-Meneses, E. & Vázquez-Cano, E. (2020). Financial technology: Review of trends, approaches and management. *Mathematics*, 8(6), 951.

Abubakar Aliyu, A. & Tasmin, B.H. (2012). The impact of information and communication technology on banks' performance and customer service delivery in the banking industry. *International Journal of Finance, Insurance and Risk Management*, 2(1), 80–90.

Adero, F.A. & Odiyo, W.O. (2020). Employee characteristics, contemporary human resource management practices and organization effectiveness. *International Journal of Business Management, Entrepreneurship and Innovation*, 2(2), 1–18.

Alegre, I., Berbegal-Mirabent, J., Guerrero, A. & Mas-Machuca, M. (2018). The real mission of the mission statement: A systematic review of the literature. *Journal of Management and Organization*, 24(4), 456–473.

Banerjee, C.S., Farooq, A. & Upadhyaya, S. (2018). The relationship between dynamic capabilities, competitive advantage & organizational performance. *International Journal of Interdisciplinary Research and Innovations*, 6(3), 603–610.

Bernardo, T., Sobkowich, K.E., Forrest, R.O., Stewart, L.S., D'Agostino, M., Gutierrez, E.P. & Gillis, D. (2021). Collaborating in the time of COVID-19: The scope and scale of innovative responses to a global pandemic. *JMIR Public Health and Surveillance*, 7(2), e25935.

Brahmbhatt, D. & Shah, J. (2017). Determinants of brand equity from the consumer's perspective: A literature review. *IUP Journal of Brand Management*, 14(4), 33–46.

Bussmann, K.D. & Niemeczek, A. (2019). Compliance through company culture and values: An international study based on the example of corruption prevention. *Journal of Business Ethics*, 157(3), 797–811.

Cabrera, E.M. & Mauricio, D. (2017). Factors affecting the success of women's entrepreneurship: A review of literature. *International Journal of Gender and Entrepreneurship*, 9(1), 31–65.

Christodoulou, A. & Cullinane, K. (2019). Identifying the main opportunities and challenges from the implementation of a port energy management system: A SWOT/PESTLE analysis. *Sustainability*, 11(21), 6046.

de Oliveira Santini, F., Ladeira, W.J., Pinto, D.C., Herter, M.M., Sampaio, C.H. & Babin, B.J. (2020). Customer engagement in social media: A framework and meta-analysis. *Journal of the Academy of Marketing Science*, 48(6), 1211–1228.

Dean, A.M. (2004). Rethinking customer expectations of service quality: Are call centers different? *Journal of Services Marketing*, 18(1), 60–78.

DesJardine, M.R., Zhang, M. & Shi, W. (2022). How shareholders impact stakeholder interests: A review and map for future research. *Journal of Management*, 49(1), 400–429.

França, A. & Ferreira, J. (2016). Resources and capabilities through the lens of value (co-) creation: A literature review. *International Journal of Innovation Science*, 8(3), 230–253.

Freij, Å. (2020). Using technology to support financial services regulatory compliance: Current applications and future prospects of regtech. *Journal of Investment Compliance*, 21(2/3), 181–190.

Guerras-Martín, L.Á., Madhok, A. & Montoro-Sánchez, Á. (2014). The evolution of strategic management research: Recent trends and current directions. *BRQ Business Research Quarterly*, 17(2), 69–76.

Gupta, P.D., Guha, S. & Krishnaswami, S.S. (2013). Firm growth and its determinants. *Journal of Innovation and Entrepreneurship*, 2(1), 1–14.

Håkansson, H. & Snehota, I. (1989). No business is an island: The network concept of business strategy. *Scandinavian Journal of Management*, 5(3), 187–200.

Herington, C., Johnson, L.W. & Scott, D. (2006). Internal relationships: Linking practitioner literature and relationship marketing theory. *European Business Review*, 18(5), 364–381.

Jiang, H., Luo, Y., Xia, J., Hitt, M. & Shen, J. (2022). Resource dependence theory in international business: Progress and prospects. *Global Strategy Journal*, 13(1), 3–57.

Kandiah, G. & Gossain, S. (1998). Reinventing value: The new business ecosystem. *Strategy and Leadership*, 26(5), 28–33.

Kannan, P.K., Chang, A.M. & Whinston, A.B. (2000). The internet information market: The emerging role of intermediaries. In: Shaw, M., Blanning, R., Strader, T., Whinston, A. (eds) *Handbook on Electronic Commerce*, pp. 569–590. Springer, Berlin, Heidelberg.

Kaur, T. & Zafar, S. (2014). Impact of social media on HR functions: A review. *Prabandhan: Indian Journal of Management*, 7(3), 26–34.

Kizgin, H., Dey, B.L., Dwivedi, Y.K., Hughes, L., Jamal, A., Jones, P., Kronemann, B., Laroche, M., Peñaloza, L., Richard, M.O., Rana, N.P., Romer, R., Tamilmani, K. & Williams, M.D. (2020). The impact of social media on consumer acculturation: Current challenges, opportunities, and an agenda for research and practice. *International Journal of Information Management*, 51, 102026.

Kumar, B. & Sharma, A. (2022). Examining the research on social media in business-to-business marketing with a focus on sales and the selling process. *Industrial Marketing Management*, 102, 122–140.

Likoko, E. & Kini, J. (2017). Inclusive business—a business approach to development. *Current Opinion in Environmental Sustainability, Inclusive Business*, 24, 84–88.

Mason, K.J. & Harris, L.C. (2006). Market orientation emphases: An exploration of macro, meso and micro drivers. *Marketing Intelligence and Planning*, 24(6), 552–571.

Molinaro, M. & Orzes, G. (2022). From forest to finished products: The contribution of Industry 4.0 technologies to the wood sector. *Computers in Industry*, 138, 103637.

Niemelä, K.M. (2020). Literature review on micro and macro factors of change in servitization-How could companies facilitate the change towards digital servitization? https://um.fi/URN:NBN:fi-fe 2020100176361.

Nwanji, T.I. & Howell, K.E. (2007). Shareholdership, stakeholdership and the modern global business environment: A survey of the literature. *Journal of Interdisciplinary Economics*, 18(4), 347–361.

Potočnik, K., Anderson, N.R., Born, M., Kleinmann, M. & Nikolaou, I. (2021). Paving the way for research in recruitment and selection: Recent developments, challenges and future opportunities. *European Journal of Work and Organizational Psychology*, 30(2), 159–174.

Qudrat-Ullah, H. & Szulanski, F. (2022). Characteristics and capabilities of a successful supplier: A conceptual model. In: Qudrat-Ullah, H. (ed.) *Understanding the Dynamics of New Normal for Supply Chains*, pp. 27–51. Springer, Cham.

Sapovadia, V. (2015). Analyzing challenges & opportunities of Ethiopian SMEs: Micro & macro economic drivers. https://mpra.ub.umi-muenchen.de/68778.

Shivdasani, A. & Zenner, M. (2004). Best practices in corporate governance: What two decades of research reveals. *Journal of Applied Corporate Finance*, 16(2–3), 29–41.

Statista. (2022). Retail e-commerce sales worldwide from 2014 to 2026. Available at: https://www.statista.com/statistics/379046/worldwide-retail-e-commerce-sales/ [Accessed: 21/12/2022].

Virtanen, Y., Jiang, Y., You, W. & Cai, H.H. (2022). International intermediaries: A systematic literature review and research agenda. *European Management Journal*. https://doi.org/10.10106/j.emj.2022.11.005.

Vrontis, D., Siachou, E., Sakka, G., Chatterjee, S., Chaudhuri, R. & Ghosh, A. (2022). Societal effects of social media in organizations: Reflective points deriving from a systematic literature review and a bibliometric meta-analysis. *European Management Journal*, 40(2), 151–162.

Werle, M. & Laumer, S. (2022). Competitor identification: A review of use cases, data sources, and algorithms. *International Journal of Information Management*, 65, 102507.

Wilkinson, I., Young, L. & Freytag, P.V. (2005). Business mating: Who chooses and who gets chosen? *Industrial Marketing Management*, 34(7), 669–680.

Yiu, D.W., Lu, Y., Bruton, G.D. & Hoskisson, R.E. (2007). Business groups: An integrated model to focus future research. *Journal of Management Studies*, 44(8), 1551–1579.

Yoon, C., Moon, S. & Lee, H. (2022). Symbiotic relationships in business ecosystem: A systematic literature review. *Sustainability*, 14(4), 2252.

Zhang, Y. (2015). The impact of brand image on consumer behavior: A literature review. *Open Journal of Business and Management*, 3(1), 58–62.

Case Study: Leading Change: A Conversation with Ron Williams

Williams' case study begins in 2001 when he arrived to find a corporation (Aetna) in need of change – having lost $280 million in the past year. He diagnosed key areas of failure and opportunity in Aetna's vast enterprise: orchestrating medical, dental, and other health and insurance benefits in a network of 843 thousand healthcare professionals with 37 million members. Williams shaped a path to recovery, focusing on a better understanding of Aetna's current customers, from small employers to the largest corporations, and the best way of expanding into new markets such as retailers, banks, and law firms. To do this, Aetna needed to build products and services suited for those groups, and Williams' strategy involved developing integrated information systems for both employers and consumers, to ensure cost-effective and high-quality healthcare delivery. Williams repeatedly made the case for this new strategy directly with Aetna's staff. He pressed the issue of values: integrity, employee engagement, excellent service, and high-quality healthcare, and conducted employee surveys and biannual performance reviews. Employees were invited to answer whether they believed their supervisors held to Aetna's values and whether they were proud to be working with the company. Williams has noted a marked improvement in responses over just a few years. External benchmarks reflect positive growth as well: Aetna has reached the number one spot as Fortune Magazine's most admired healthcare company, after once occupying the bottom position. Williams invested a great deal in technology which he believes will "shape the future of health care." He describes a Care Engine, containing an individual member's health record and up-to-the-minute journal information and health guidelines that are "converted into computer algorithms." This system can detect and fill gaps in care for patient conditions that go undetected, tests that should be administered, and medicine that should not be prescribed. Williams has also given consumers the ability to find and compare the costs of tests and doctor visits. He believes the company can check the trillions of dollars in healthcare spending through smart technology. For him, healthcare reform means we "get and keep everyone covered; maintain the employer-based system ... reorient the system toward prevention, value, and quality of care; and use market incentives to improve coverage, drive down costs and make the system more consumer-oriented."

Chapter Questions

1. What is the business environment and why do organisations analyse it?
2. How can businesses exploit internal factors to ensure stability?
3. How responsive should businesses be to events in the external environment?
4. List and describe common approaches to environmental analysis and what tools are typically used to analyse the macro-environment, micro-environment, and internal environments.

Chapter 2

Forms of Business Ownership

Learning Outcomes

By the end of this chapter, you will be able to:

- identify the different types of business forms.
- describe the characteristics and structure of the types of business forms.
- state the advantages and disadvantages of the types of business forms.

Chapter Outline

- Introduction
- Sole Proprietorship (Advantages and Disadvantages)
- Partnerships (Advantages and Disadvantages)
- Limited Liability Company (Advantages and Disadvantages)
- Business Corporations (Advantages and Disadvantages)
- Cooperative Societies
- Social Enterprises
- Conclusion
- References
- Chapter Question
- Sources

2.1 Introduction

Prior to making a decision to start an enterprise, certain critical decisions must be taken. One of these is the decision on what form of organisation

 DOI: 10.4324/9781003458524-2

the business must adopt. Business organisation take different forms; it may be unincorporated examples of which include sole proprietorships and partnerships and incorporated with examples as limited liability companies (private or public), limited liability partnerships, and limited partnerships (Al-Darayseh & Waples, 1993; Chen, 2022). Other business forms include business trusts as well as social enterprises which have emerged as a popular business-charity venture in the past decade (Galera & Borzaga, 2009). It is worth noting that all these forms of businesses differ in relation to each other in many ways, including the procedures of organisation, management and control, taxation, governing law, and continuity of legal existence which is critical for the sustainability of the business, personal liability of the owners, and transferability of interests in the business (Al-Darayseh & Waples, 1993).

In the process of deciding the ownership structure to adopt, the process should examine pertinent issues in the form of business goals such as start-up cost minimisation, desired levels of control and responsibility for operating the business, sources of funding, and the level of involvement by other people to complement the skills set of the business owners (Frazer, 2015). Other critical considerations may include profit-making and retention policies; the position of the business on paying either business or personal tax on profit made, as well as liability exposure (Allen et al., 2022). Most importantly, the risk threshold of the business owners needs to be determined since each ownership structure comes with its own forms of risk and features (Rexer & Sheehan, 1994). Considering these issues thoroughly would help determine the most suitable type of business to adopt when one is ready to set up a business venture. The different forms of business setups have been explored in the next sections.

2.2 Sole Proprietorship

A sole proprietorship is deemed the simplest, least expensive, most common, and oldest form of business structure globally, as the people and financial resources required for this setup is not as difficult in acquiring as compared to other forms of business setups (Akbar et al., 2017). A sole proprietorship can also be termed as a sole trade organisation or individual proprietorship. A sole proprietorship is a form of business organisation in which a single individual owns and makes decisions for the business, is self-employed, and therefore engages in the business alone and enjoys the full profit and liability associated with running the business (Hogarth-Scott et al, 1996). Should there be any losses beyond the business' capital, the personal assets of the sole proprietor may be used to cover up business losses. Legally, there is no distinction between the owner and the business; thus, to put it in layman's terms, the individual is the business and the business is that individual; neither is there any dichotomy between the business and management. The business owner is responsible for sourcing capital to establish and run the business. In the formation of a sole proprietorship, the individual or business owner may decide to use his or her true name and will not have to go through any legal registration process (Gustafson, 2004). However, the business owner would need to go through legal registration if he or she decides to use any other name aside from his name, initials, or surname. This legal process grants the individual the legal right to the registered business name. It is however important to note that the legal formalities for this form of business setup are very minimal and sometimes even nonexistent.

The sole proprietor does not require any filing or formal document to create this business and has complete control over the day-to-day running of the business. No other person has any right to participate in management, though the business owner may assign authority to agents or employees through a contract. Again, a sole proprietor would not be liable to share profits but is liable for losses of the enterprise. Taxes paid from the business is deemed as that of the individual because the profit from the business is perceived as the personal income of the business owner (Briggeman & Akers, 2010). The sole proprietor is not liable to prepare an audited account or financial statement of their business or even divulge the financial status of the business to any organisation as part of a regulatory requirement. The individual is also accountable for personal offences committed by himself or his employees within the purview of the terms of employment. The sole proprietor is normally advised to keep a business account separate from his or her personal account to avoid possible financial impropriety to the detriment of the business. The business terminates when the sole proprietor dies or ends the business. Technically, sole proprietorships have no guarantee for continuity of existence; however, the enterprise of a sole proprietor could be passed on to other persons either family related or to anyone.

2.2.1 Advantages of Sole Proprietorship

Sole proprietorships are comparatively easier to form, and the owners have singular and absolute ownership and control of the business and all its profits as aforementioned. The owner of the business is also accountable for all the operational activities of the business, and his privacy is secured without any external interference. This form of business organisation is characterised by low start-up capital and costs with minimal regulation control. The owner also enjoys some tax concessions, where the income of the proprietor is taxed only once as it occurs in some jurisdictions (Anie, 2022). The business can also be managed by the owner in the way he chooses with so much flexibility. Closing down the business is also as easy as the formation of the business. The business does not require any permit to close down, and it can be done at any time. As the business expands, the legal structure can be changed easily. The sole proprietor is the only knowledge holder of the secrets of the business and maintains a high level of privacy, thereby deciding whether to divulge the financial position of the business or not (Byrd & Richey, 1998).

2.2.2 *Disadvantages of Sole Proprietorship*

Sole proprietorships have some demerits. The proprietor is individually responsible for all the losses and liabilities of the business; hence, should there be a lawsuit against the business, the entire personal and business assets of the owner, including his personal accounts, could be made accessible to the creditor or claimant if the accounts of the business are unable to cover the debt (Vargas-Hernández and Noruzi, 2010). This puts the assets of the business owner at risk and exposes the business to huge unlimited liability and legal responsibility. In the absence of the business owner, the business ceases to exist unless a proper succession plan is put in place. Typically, when the business owner passes or suffers incapacitation at a point, the business also dies. In terms of funding, the business is solely financed by the business owner, which slows down the expansion of the business. The business owner's responsibility of taking decisions and executing every activity concerning the business daily is tough and challenging as the individual is expected to play multiple roles of management, finance, marketing, and human resource development (Dang & Sharma, 2015). The strengths, weaknesses, and management capabilities of the owner are also brought to bear on the business. Employee retention is also difficult as they come and leave at will. In relation to taxation, the sole proprietor bears the tax burden alone because he is the sole taxpayer, and raising capital to fund and expand the activities of the business is most nonviable (Dey, 2018). The sole proprietor may also be deficient in some areas of the business because they may not possess all the requisite skills needed to manage the business.

In most cases, setting up the appropriate infrastructure, attracting the right calibre of people, and remunerating them adequately are also huge challenges (Szaban, 2018).

2.3 Partnerships

A partnership is an association of two or more people who operate a business as co-owners for profit (Graen & Hui, 1996). The profit and management of the business are shared by all the partners who have unlimited liability and generally depend on the financial support and entrepreneurial skills of at least two individuals. In Ghana, partnerships are incorporated under the "Incorporated Private Partnerships Act" of 1962 (Act 152). Partnerships may be formed in two ways: either by the conduct of the parties or by agreement, express, or implied. While it is usually not necessary to provide a written agreement to create a partnership, the basic requirement is to describe the duties and rights of the partners to each other in the form of a written agreement. Alternatively, each of the partners is deemed to have the same voice in the control and management of their partnership, and hence, should there be any disagreement, a majority of the partners, in terms of numbers, have a significant amount of controls in the business. This general rule could be revised by agreement (Bull et al., 2009). For the registration of the partnership, the partners are mandated to produce a copy of the partnership agreement in addition to completing a registration form obtained from the Registrar General's Department (for instance in Ghana) or Company House (for instance in the UK), signed by all partners, and may vary per country. Each of the partners in a partnership has complete individual liability for the entire partnership responsibilities. However, all the partners are severally and jointly accountable for any damages caused by an offence or a breach of trust by each partner in the space of the partnership, as well as being jointly liable for all additional partnership obligations (Byrd & Richey, 1998).

Forming a partnership is more intricate than forming a sole proprietorship, and the cost differs according to size and complexity. A group of people may form a basic modest partnership without the assistance of an accountant or lawyer although it is better to seek professional advice. In Ghana, persons allowed to form a partnership must not exceed 20 in number; must be above 18 years; and of sound mind, free of guilt of any offence relating to dishonesty or fraud within the five years prior to the formation of the agreement (RGD-Ghana, 2019). A corporate organisation cannot be part of a partnership but could go into a joint venture. Partners make joint decisions about the business while sharing its profits and losses. After incorporation, unlike a sole proprietorship, a partnership becomes legally distinct from its partners. Similar to the mode of taxation for a sole proprietorship, each partner is taxed individually per their portion of profits, and the partnership does not incur any extra tax burden. Partners can however be sued individually in relation to the obligations and debts of the business. They could also be sued jointly with the other business partners or with the business. Sleeping partners within the partnership may be inactive in the management of the business but have equal responsibilities and liabilities with the other partners. This is also known as limited partnership (Milman, 2017). The liabilities of the partners are restricted only to the extent of the sum of their investment in the business. The partnership is required by law to prepare financial statements and file with the Registrar General's Department but under no obligation to have the statement audited or released to the public (RGD-Ghana, 2019).

Similar to sole proprietorship, partnerships do not exist perpetually. For instance, a partner can opt out or be disinterested in the business venture. Aside from that a partner's interest in the partnership in terms of their separate shares of profits and partnership capital can be allocated. One observation worth noting is that the assignment of rights in partnerships does not allow the assignee the right to administer or manage the business or to request any transaction account of the partnership information or to check the books of the partnership (Al-Darayseh & Waples, 1993). The rights of the assignee just enable them to receive the profits the assigning partner would have received, per the contract.

2.3.1 Advantages of Partnerships

Like sole proprietorships, partnerships also have several advantages. The formation of a partnership is quite easy with low start-up costs. A group of people with similar interests can come together to form a partnership and thus eases the burden of raising capital by one person as is the case in sole proprietorships. Each of the partners contributes their quota to the capital requirement needs of the business and applies their personal assets, skills, and resources to the use and benefit of the business, for instance, in securing bank loans. Management of the business is more dispersed among the partners, unlike the centralised decision-making structure of sole proprietorships. Regulation is also minimal with some tax benefits. Succession is much more assured since the partners could decide to legally allow the business to exist should any of the partners pass on or in their absence (Asghar, 2016).

2.3.2 *Disadvantages of Partnership*

Unlike a sole proprietorship, partners in a partnership propose differing views as to the way the business should be operated. This could culminate in division and dissension which may not augur well for the business, if consensus and harmony are not reached. In a partnership, it is mandatory that profits are shared even if some partners may be deemed to be undeserving of their profits for varying reasons. On the other hand, other partners may also feel they deserve more profits than they are given due to their exceptional performance although the contract may stipulate clear guidance for profit sharing. Other disagreements may arise in decision-making due to the divergent views and perceptions of the partners on issues relating to the business. Another disadvantage of a partnership is that every partner is responsible for their own liabilities or deeds as well as the liabilities of the other partners; thus, the unlimited liability feature of partnerships is also evident. Decision-making in partnership is decentralised and open to all partners to share their views for consensus building on pertinent issues. If some partners decide to hold back and refuse to cooperate, not much progress would be made in advancing the cause and course of the business (Kashyap & Kashyap, 2010). Again, when all the partners empty their coffers to raise initial capital to start the business, raising extra capital subsequently becomes a bit challenging. There could also be repercussive issues in respect to the sharing of profit. As such, the mode for sharing profits and ploughing back profits into the business must be documented early on in the business setup process to avoid unwarranted incidents. Divided and unclear authority in the form of organisational structures could give rise to misunderstanding where individual partners arrogate to themselves powers that they are not eligible to have or do not belong to them. Conflict among partners is inevitable and could be pervasive if not controlled. In a partnership, it is often challenging to find suitable, committed partners who would protect the interest of the business as in the instance of sole proprietorships. Hence, the continuity of the business may hang in the balance unless issues like this are thoroughly discussed and finalised by partners (Ray, 2012).

2.4 Limited Liability Company

A limited liability company (LLC) is a type of legal entity, typically organised under a state law that offers limited liability to all its owners. "Limited liability" here indicates that the individual shareholders are limited in liability to their contribution of investment and therefore cannot be held responsible for the debts and other additional commitments of the company (Akey and Appel, 2021). LLC possesses unique features including the fact that it is an amalgamation of the limited liability structure of legal corporations and a favourable tax regime as well as the operational flexibility of legal partnership organisations. LLCs exercise legal authority almost like that of corporations and are entitled to own any amount or the entire stock in a corporation. Where the law allows, LLC could also be adopted by professional businesses like medicine and law in the instance where "pass-through" tax implications and limited liability are necessary. Sole proprietorships and partnerships can migrate to become LLCs. The members of the LLC could contribute tangible, intangible, or any other property that would be beneficial to the organisation including money, services performed, and promissory notes, among others as their share to the business (Cebriá, 2023). The members may even be sleeping partners who may invest in the business but may not participate actively in the operations or day-to-day running of the business.

2.4.1 Advantages of Limited Liability Companies

One key advantage of the LLC is that liability is limited to the amount contributed or to the tune of the shares acquired by each shareholder and has no "double taxation" (Mancuso, 2021). In other words, if the shareholder has made full payment for their shares, they are by no means responsible for the debts of the company. When one begins to conduct business as a limited liability company, one's professional status and reputation increase significantly. A limited company, unlike a sole proprietorship, is a legal "person" with a completely separate identity from its owners and directors. Consequently, corporations can enter into contracts in their own names and are accountable for their own debts and liabilities. The professional status of a limited liability company will add prestige and credibility to your company (Burduli & Chitashvili, 2020). In fact, some businesses and organisations (particularly in the IT, finance, and construction industries) are only willing to work with other corporations. Typically, this is due to the level of risk associated with the contracts they award. Comparatively, partnerships are not expensive to set up as it has just a few statutory regulations to grapple with. Again, a partnership is a hub of multiple talents with individuals who have key skills pertinent to the business (Feldman, 2021). The partners also pool financial resources together to fund the business. Given the number of people involved in a partnership, succession is not a challenge since the partners could legally establish the continuity of the business. Aside from the individual taxes paid by partners, no other taxes are levied on them.

2.4.2 *Disadvantages of Limited Liability Companies*

The fees and taxes associated with the business structure are the primary disadvantages of limited liability companies. Despite the fact that owners of a limited liability company avoid double taxation, they must pay self-employment taxes. The owner pays these taxes twice because he or she is both the employee and the employer (Gup & Beekarry, 2009). Generally, a limited liability company has the same two funding options as a corporation: equity and debt. Fundraising via the equity route involves selling ownership stakes in the business. This will also necessitate the addition of one or more members to the list of members. Thus, you will have one or more additional members to share your profits with (Toson, 2020). Existing members might be required to share decision-making authority with the new member. Avoiding this course of action will necessitate the members' difficult search for an investor.

2.5 Business Corporations

A business corporation is a large and limited liability company which can either be private or public and headed by a board of directors who are not part of the day-to-day running of the corporation and may or may not have an interest in the corporation. Through a process termed as an initial public offering (IPO), corporations float their shares to the public opening it up to a wider financial market and presence (Ibbotson & Ritter, 1995). As the presence of the board of directors is imperative to this business structure, the primary responsibility of the Board is to make policy decisions for the corporation through the development of strategic goals for which the management is liable to execute. The Board is also responsible for recruiting and appraising the performance of the chief executive officer and other functions left to the Board to decide (Ong & Wan, 2001). Additionally, the Board ensures the approval of the distribution of shareholders' income, also known as dividends as well as other approvals that are deemed fit for the Board. A business corporation is owned by shareholders who gain ownership through the purchase of shares as their part of the investment and enjoy limited liability to the number of shares purchased. It can be in existence perpetually with the terms and conditions on the transfer of interests by shareholders (Rafique, 2011). As a legal entity, the corporation shares similar features with limited liability companies including separation from its shareholders, buy and sell assets, go into binding contracts, be held liable for its activities and actions, prosecute and be prosecuted, and is liable to be taxed as well (Venter & De Clercq, 2007).

2.5.1 Advantages of Business Corporations

Business corporations offer some advantages, including greater access to financial resources, limited liability for shareholders, specialised management, and business continuity. Most big and small businesses alike potentially venture into business corporations as they grow and expand. The managers of the corporation administer the instructions of the Board, while the shareholders have the responsibility to elect the members of the Board to run the corporation's business. The traditional roles of the shareholders may also vary as a result of bylaws and distinct agreements among them, including voting rights or voting agreements and articles of organisation (Sharvani, 2011). Shareholders are only liable to the amount of shares purchased with a high level of transparency and accountability in the financial administration of the business. The annual general meetings (AGMs) attended by the shareholders offer opportunities for them to share their views and register their displeasure of a Board or management decision, making the decision-making process in corporations very robust and effective (Jhunjhunwala, 2011). A corporation usually enjoys longevity and the incapacitation or death of a shareholder does not end the life of the corporation. Shares of a business's corporate stock can be transferred on the terms set out in the agreements signed by the parties involved. One key advantage of an incorporated business is that it is able to secure funds through the sale of shares to the public to facilitate the operations of the business which offers competitive advantages for this type of business setup. Funds can also be secured by borrowing from the bank and other local and international financial institutions. Given the financial position of the corporation, it is able to hire experts who bring in their expertise to enhance the corporation's operations and performance (Cooke et al., 2019).

2.5.2 *Disadvantages of Business Corporations*

The huge setup cost for a corporation is quite daunting. This may include fees for licensing, filing, other documentation, and standard protocols. Managers of a corporation may not be shareholders of the corporation; on the other hand, the shareholders may not necessarily work in the corporation (DesJardine et al., 2023). This is likely to reduce the level of commitment from both parties, eliciting several other challenges. Again, the interests and priorities of these two groups may differ; while the shareholders are primarily keeping an eye on dividends, they may do this at the detriment of employee welfare and vice versa. The regulatory obligations of corporations and government's supervisory responsibilities may place undue pressure on small corporations (Atal, 2022). Another disadvantage is the issue of "double taxation" where both the corporation and the shareholders pay taxes on their revenue and dividends respectively to the state.

2.6 Cooperatives

A cooperative is an association set up to provide a service or services for its members and is typically made up of members who share particular characteristics or interests, such as same employer, trade, or profession (Mordhorst & Jensen, 2019). It is also called a "co-op" or cooperative society in some jurisdictions such as the United Kingdom. Cooperatives are member-owned, controlled, and operated businesses that fulfil their members' economic, social, and cultural needs and aspirations. Cooperatives bring individuals together in a democratic and egalitarian manner. Cooperatives are democratically run according to the principle of "one member, one vote," regardless of whether the members are customers, employees, users, or residents (Saz-Gil et al., 2021). Members have equal voting rights regardless of the amount of capital they have contributed to the organisation. Cooperatives, as businesses motivated by values in addition to profit, adhere to internationally accepted principles and collaborate to build a better world. Putting fairness, equality, and social justice at the core of the enterprise, cooperatives allow people to work together to create sustainable businesses that generate long-term employment and prosperity (Imaz & Eizagirre, 2020). Since cooperatives are not owned by shareholders, the economic and social benefits of their activities remain in the communities in which they are founded. Profits are either reinvested in the business or distributed to the members (Bijman & Wijers, 2019).

2.7 Social Enterprises

Social enterprises are businesses that prioritise people and the environment over shareholder profit. These organisations are motivated by a social or environmental mission and reinvest their profits in fostering positive social change. Social enterprises pledge to reinvest the majority of their profits or surpluses in achieving their social or environmental goals (Sikandar, Kohar & Salam, 2020). This is a fundamental distinction between social enterprises and conventional businesses, which are accountable to shareholders and are thus primarily motivated by their interests. Social enterprises and business corporations are frequently confused. While business corporations are typically shareholder-driven organisations, social enterprises exist to generate social value (de Souza João-Roland & Granados, 2020). Profitability is important to social enterprises, but it is not their primary objective. Where social enterprises do pay shareholder dividends, the proportion is capped at 49 per cent of total profits, ensuring that the majority of profits are available to support the enterprise's social mission. Social enterprises are autonomous businesses, free from state or government control. They are owned and managed with the organisation's social/environmental mission in mind (Kimura et al., 2019). The majority of a social enterprise's revenue should come from trading (goods/services, contracts, and service level agreements), as opposed to grants and other forms of funding. Businesses with a social and/or environmental mission should be transparent about their efforts to achieve their goals (Chaudhuri et al., 2020). They should be able to demonstrate the social impact they have had and how profits or surpluses were invested to achieve this. In the event of company dissolution, social enterprises commit to distributing assets to achieve social and environmental objectives (García-Jurado, Pérez-Barea & Nova, 2021). A clause in the governing documents enshrines this commitment to prevent the distribution of residual assets for private gain, e.g., in the event that a social enterprise is acquired by new owners.

2.8 Conclusion

From the sections discussed, it is evident that different forms of business ownership exist with different characteristics, structures, and functions. These include sole proprietorship, partnership, limited liability companies, business corporations, cooperatives, and social enterprises. Prior to making a decision to form a business, one of the huge factors to be considered is to decide the form the business will assume. This is not a straightforward decision because several factors need to be accounted for in order to arrive at such a decision. These factors include risk affinity, governing laws, resources, objectives for setting up the business, tax regimen, owner liability, and transferability of interest, among others. Hence, potential business owners need to study these factors extensively in order to choose, bearing in mind the pros and cons of each business structure.

The onset of the COVID-19 pandemic led to a level of restriction in the movement of individuals, restrictions were imposed on movement to offices, and this resulted in the automation of several activities, including the automation of registration of businesses. Currently, people can apply electronically for opening of businesses as opposed to the in-person registration, with its numerous challenges. Time for registration of businesses has been reduced significantly, and it is expected that entrepreneurs will take advantage of the revised business registration procedures to open more businesses. Again, the onset of the COVID-19 pandemic led to a number of businesses retrenching its employees. With these experiences, a number of individuals have moved into setting up their own business, be it sole proprietorship, partnership, and in some instances, limited liability companies. Thus, even though the COVID-19 pandemic is seen in the negative perspective, it has caused persons to be innovative and set up their own businesses.

References

Akbar, F., Omar, A., Wadood, F. & Al-Subari, S. N. A. (2017). The importance of SMES, and furniture manufacturing SMES in Malaysia: A review of literature. *International Journal of Business Management*, 2(4), 119–130.

Akey, P. and Appel, I. 2021. The limits of limited liability: Evidence from industrial pollution. *The Journal of Finance*, 76(1), 5–55.

Al-Darayseh, M. M. & Waples, E. (1993). Startup businesses – selecting the right form: Tax and limited liability factors. *Management Research News*, 16(2/3), 19–22.

Allen, E. J., Allen, J. C., Raghavan, S. & Solomon, D. H. (2022). On the tax efficiency of startup firms. *Review of Accounting Studies*, 1–42.

Anie, D. P. V. S. (2022). Opportunities and challenges of one person company for micro and Small Enterprises in Indonesia. *Corporate and Trade Law Review*, 2(1), 80–95.

Asghar, M. S. (2016). Limited liability partnership in Pakistan: An overview. Available at SSRN 2792534.

Atal, M. R. (2022). Globalizing regulation: A new progressive agenda for trade and investment. *Global Perspectives*, 3(1), 39794.

Bijman, J. & Wijers, G. (2019). Exploring the inclusiveness of producer cooperatives. *Current Opinion in Environmental Sustainability*, 41, 74–79.

Briggeman, B. C. & Akers, M. M. (2010). The credit advantage of farm and rural small business ownership. *Agricultural Finance Review*, 70(3), 353–364.

Bull, N., Nelson, S. & Fisher, R. (2009). Characteristics of business ownership: Overview for pass-through entities and evidence on S corporate ownership from linked data. In *Proceedings Annual Conference on Taxation and Minutes of the Annual Meeting of the National Tax Association* (Vol. 102, pp. 37–49). National Tax Association.

Burduli, I. & Chitashvili, N. (2020). Expulsion of a shareholder from a limited liability company on substantial grounds. *TalTech Journal of European Studies*, 10(2), 7–27.

Byrd, S. & Richey, B. (1998). The choice of entity for the small business owner. *The Mid-Atlantic Journal of Business*, 34(3), 205–234.

Cebriá, L. H. (2023). Introduction to the law of benefit corporations and other public purpose-driven companies. In: Henry, P., Carlos, V. V., Jaime, A. S. (eds) *The International Handbook of Social Enterprise Law*, pp. 301–317. Springer, Switzerland

Chaudhuri, R., Vrontis, D., Chavan, G. & Shams, S. R. (2020). Social business enterprises as a research domain: A bibliometric analysis and research direction. *Journal of Social Entrepreneurship*, 119, 1–15.

Chen, F. (2022). An overview of business entities in the market. In: *Essential Knowledge and Legal Practices for Establishing and Operating Companies in China*, 3–8. Springer, Singapore.

Cooke, F. L., Wood, G., Wang, M. & Veen, A. (2019). How far has international HRM travelled? A systematic review of literature on multinational corporations (2000–2014). *Human Resource Management Review*, 29(1), 59–75.

Dang, R. & Sharma, N. (2015). One person company: Concept, opportunities & challenges in India. *International Journal for Research in Management and Pharmacy*, 4(3), 1–4.

de Souza João-Roland, I. & Granados, M. L. (2020). Social innovation drivers in social enterprises: Systematic review. *Journal of Small Business and Enterprise Development*, 27(5), 775–795.

DesJardine, M. R., Zhang, M. & Shi, W. (2023). How shareholders impact stakeholder interests: A review and map for future research. *Journal of Management*, 49(1), 400–429.

Dey, P. K. (2018). One-person company a new business opportunity in new companies act: A panorama. *International Journal for Advance Research and Development*, 3(3), 10–14.

Feldman, E. R. (2021). The corporate parenting advantage, revisited. *Strategic Management Journal*, 42(1), 114–143.

Frazer, L. (2015). Failure to launch. *The CPA Journal*, 85(5), 34–36.

Galera, G. & Borzaga, C. (2009). Social enterprise: An international overview of its conceptual evolution and legal implementation. *Social Enterprise Journal*, 5(3), 210–228.

García-Jurado, A., Pérez-Barea, J. J. & Nova, R. J. (2021). A new approach to social entrepreneurship: A systematic review and meta-analysis. *Sustainability*, 13(5), 2754.

Graen, G. & Hui, C. (1996). Managing changes in globalizing business: How to manage cross-cultural business partners. *Journal of Organizational Change Management*, 9(3), 62–72.

Gup, B. E. & Beekarry, N. (2009). Limited liability companies (LLCs) and financial crimes. *Journal of Money Laundering Control*, 12(1), 7–18.

Gustafson, C. R. (2004). Rural small business finance: Evidence from the 1998 survey of small business finances. *Agricultural Finance Review*, 64(1), 33–43.

Hogarth-Scott, S., Watson, K. & Wilson, N. (1996). Do small businesses have to practise marketing to survive and grow? *Marketing Intelligence and Planning*, 14(1), 6–18.

Ibbotson, R. G. & Ritter, J. R. (1995). Initial public offerings. *Handbooks in Operations Research and Management Science*, 9, 993–1016.

Imaz, O. & Eizagirre, A. (2020). Responsible innovation for sustainable development goals in business: An agenda for cooperative firms. *Sustainability*, 12(17), 6948.

Jhunjhunwala, S. (2011). Shareholders' rights–an overview. *Indian Journal of Corporate Governance*, 4(2), 47–51.

Kashyap, D. & Kashyap, A. K. (2010). Limited liability partnership as advantage to small business: Indian scenario. In *National Seminar, Emerging Issues in Commerce and Management*. SSRN. https://doi.org/10.2139/ssrn.1545766.

Kimura, F., Hagihara, K., Horie, N. & Asahi, C. (2019). Types of social enterprises and various social problems. In: Asahi, C. (ed.) *Building Resilient Regions*. New Frontiers in Regional Science: Asian Perspectives, vol 35. 107–124. Springer, Singapore.

Mancuso, A. (2021). Form your own limited liability company, In: Christine, M. (ed.) *Create an LLC in Any State*. Nolo.

Milman, D. (2017). A review of developments in partnership law 2017. *Sweet and Maxwell's Company Law Newsletter*, 399, 1–5.

Mordhorst, M. & Jensen, K. (2019). Co-operatives. In: Teresa, S. L., Christina, L., Heidi, J.S. T. (eds) *The Routledge Companion to the Makers of Global Business*, 217–233. New York

Ong, C. H. & Wan, T. W. D. (2001). Board structure, board process and board performance: A review & research agenda. *Journal of Comparative International Management*, 4(1), 1–25.

Rafique, Z. (2011). Rethinking of rights and procedural complexity in transfer of share: A review under company law in Bangladesh. *Journal of Advanced Research in Law and Economics (JARLE)*, 2(03), 60–77.

Ray, D. (2012). The emergence of limited liability partnerships. Available at SSRN 2117240.

Registrar-General department (RGD) RGD-Ghana. (2019). *Incorporation of Partnership.* Available at: https://rgd.gov.gh/partnership.html [Accessed: 10/01/2023].

Rexer, C. & Sheehan, T. J. (1994). Organizing the firm: Choosing the right business entity. *Journal of Applied Corporate Finance*, 7(1), 59–65.

Saz-Gil, I., Bretos, I. & Díaz-Foncea, M. (2021). Cooperatives and social capital: A narrative literature review and directions for future research. *Sustainability*, 13(2), 534.

Sharvani, B. (2011). OECD principles on shareholder rights: (summary of the Principle II and III of OECD principles of corporate governance). *Indian Journal of Corporate Governance*, 4(2), 52–59.

Sikandar, H., Kohar, U. H. A. & Salam, S. (2020). The evolution of social innovation and its global research trends: A bibliometric analysis. *Systematic Literature Review and Meta-Analysis Journal*, 1(2), 117–133.

Szaban, J. (2018). Self-employment and entrepreneurship: A theoretical approach. *Central European Management Journal*, 26(2), 89–120.

Toson, S. J. (2020). Truth revealed: Challenging the mythical narrative of the low-profit limited liability company. *Social Business.* https://doi.org/10.1362/204440821X16206324311114.

Venter, J. M. P. & De Clercq, B. (2007). A three-sector comparative study of the impact of taxation on small and medium enterprises. *Meditari Accountancy Research*, 15(2), 131–151. https://doi.org/10.1362/204440821X16206324311114.

Vargas-Hernández, J.G. and Noruzi, M.R. (2010). A literature review of partnerships. *Journal of US-China Public Administration*, 7(10), 60–96.

Chapter Questions

Read each of the following cases and determine the form of business ownership that applies to each case.

1. As a young child, Karina had a passion for the welfare of animals. After she graduated from college, Karina landed a job in an organisation whose mission is to produce and sell a variety of animal foods and use the proceeds to create public awareness about endangered animals

while providing shelter and care for rescued animals. Karina's employer depends largely on these proceeds to fund its business activities.

2. Kyle and Palo had been friends for a long time. The friends shared a common interest in computer technology. Kyle had done some software design and computer work on his own for neighbours and family friends. It wasn't long before he realised that there was a demand for small businesses to have affordable computer consultants. He decided to start a business. Kyle discussed his venture with Palo and asked him if he would like to combine capital and take an active role in the business with him. Both Kyle and Palo are equally responsible for the businesses' risks and rewards.

3. Rachel worked in one of her family's two furniture stores. When her grandfather decided to expand the business and build three more stores, Rachel realised that he would need a lot of capital to get the construction started. She suggested that her grandfather raise the money by selling shares of stock in the company to just a few people, not to the general public. He sold 1,000 shares of stock to 100 people and kept 1,500 shares.

4. Doug grew up on a large farm in southwest Wisconsin. As a college graduation gift, Doug's father gave him several hundred acres of land to raise organic soybeans, grain, and corn. Doug works the fields by himself, negotiates deals with buyers, repairs equipment, and handles all the accounting and financial issues for the business he has named The Natural Element.

5. Ming was an associate orthodontist in a large dental practice. While attending a professional seminar, Ming ran into a former colleague, Kevin. He told Ming that he and five others were planning to open their own dental practice. They were looking for an orthodontist to include in their practice. Within three months, six members of the dental practice filed the necessary paperwork and paid annual fees to the government to start their new dental practice. Before they open for business,

they will have to make sure that each member has sufficient malpractice insurance.

6. Chip and Charlie own a local pizza shop. The pizza was the talk of the neighbourhood. When customers suggested that they open more stores, Chip and Charlie were hesitant. They didn't have the money. Chip and Charlie went ahead with plans to open another shop across town. To finance the venture, the partners formed a private corporation and sold shares of stock to friends. They chose a legal arrangement that allowed them to avoid dual taxation.

7. James owns part of a business. He purchased several hundred shares of stock in a large, nationally recognised steel company. Several thousand other people own stock in the company too. Each year, all the shareholders receive a detailed report about the financial activities of the company.

8. For years, Andrew worked for a national airline as a pilot. When the stress got to him, he decided to simplify his life. He packed his bags and moved to Key West. Andrew decided to start his own transportation and touring service for travellers. To accomplish his goal, he needed to purchase a small commuter plane. He only had one problem – money. Andrew telephoned his very wealthy uncle in Seattle to see if he would like a piece of the action. Andrew proposed that he would run the day-to-day activities of the company, while his uncle would just provide a percentage of the capital. His uncle agreed, and Andrew contacted an attorney to develop a written agreement.

9. Annette started working as a repairer in a local appliance store when she was in school. She loved the work and was promoted to service manager within a few years. Annette had always wanted her own business, and she started to research ways to achieve her goals. The next year, Annette opened her store, Annette's Appliance and Repair Shop. Her store is a distributor of Whirlpool washers and dryers.

10. As a successful businessperson, Ben wanted to take the next step to expand his mid-size company internationally. He knew he didn't have enough capital and know-how to get into foreign markets. He contacted a former business associate who owned a garment manufacturing company in Australia. Together, they worked out a deal that would benefit both of their companies in a relationship that would last no longer than one year.

Source: Business Ownership – Lesson and Mini Case Studies, https://wlresources.dpi.wi.gov/courseware/lesson/254/overview

Chapter 3

How to Start and Grow a Business

Learning Outcomes

By the end of this chapter, you will be able to:

- describe the steps associated with forming a business.
- describe the business growth process.
- identify the sacrifices and challenges associated with entrepreneurship.
- state the fact that the success of a business lies in the process and not the results.
- provide the personal entrepreneurial attributes essential to a business.
- describe the skill set required by every entrepreneur to run a business.
- describe the importance of bookkeeping and working with the right team.

Chapter Outline

- Introduction
- Stages in Business Formation and Growth
- Starting with the Endgame in Mind
- Preparatory Stage for Starting a Business
- Profile of an Entrepreneur
- Starting the Business

DOI: 10.4324/9781003458524-3

- Business Growth and Expansion
- Conclusion
- References
- Chapter Questions

3.1 Introduction

The number of businesses that spring up globally every year run into the hundreds of thousands as the need to meet the demands of the society keeps surging every moment (Asongu & Odhiambo, 2019). Although starting a business seems easy and simple, the viability and long-term sustainability of the business are critical questions individuals who want to start a business need to ask before they set out to start a business. The will to start a business is what births the whole debate of entrepreneurship. Entrepreneurs all over the world have led the development of several businesses, some of which have been a phenomenal success and others have suffered failures regardless of the size of the business. Initially, many businesses start off well but, over time, some either exit prematurely or hang on the flanks. The reasons behind such early exits or business failures are diverse and multifaceted. For some, it can be due to a lack of an entrepreneurial disposition, inadequate funding, lack of appropriate skill set, applying the wrong strategies, and not having the right business knowledge (Akter & Iqbal, 2020). Yet for others, it borders on their inability to seek direction and help, lack or inadequacy of technical expertise, not having a blueprint to follow, absence of mentorship, lack of industry and competitor intelligence, and copying blindly, among others. This chapter, therefore, focuses on understanding how to start and grow a business successfully.

3.2 Stages in Business Formation and Growth

There are several models and theories that have been applied to the formation and growth of businesses, regardless of how little or how big an individual would want to start. Salamzadeh and Kirby (2017), in their study, proposed a model for the process of creation and evolutionary trend of new ventures. The stages opined included venture ideation – where an idea is birthed; shaping the entrepreneurial intention – which is a critical stage as many new venture ideas never see the light of day or fail if the idea is not followed through; preparation stage – which covers resource mobilisation, activity organisation, and competence creation; networking – which is meant to leverage on relationships to facilitate entry into new markets; and the creation of value for the market along the value chain for the facilitation of the process of getting the products or services to the target market. Other studies have suggested some key factors that are vital for starting and growing businesses including availability capital, talent, expertise, technology, and a strong people resource strategy (Alpenidze et al., 2019; Hossinger et al., 2020).

Companies with better "ideas" in terms of proactivity and pragmatism on how to meet the needs of their customers are perceived to be more likely to succeed. These ideas are the solutions that are transformed into the desired products and services required by customers, which are then positioned, branded, and sold to them (Venesz, Dőry & Raišienė, 2022). Although end users or customers are served with several product alternatives in the market, product branding has several benefits as strategic selling points for products. Product branding is a source of product differentiation in the minds of the customers, which psychologically guides the decisions of customers into the choice of product they decide to spend their monies on (Mahaputra, 2021). Branding supports a high-growth business to depict an image of unique product quality to create and capitalise on the goodwill a business enjoys within the market they find themselves in (Kim & Sullivan, 2019). An important factor in the process of achieving a unique product development and brand positioning is the human resource strategy that is employed in these processes. Although it is not essentially required for entrepreneurs to have full knowledge of human resource strategy before they venture into a business, it is worth noting that a company comes alive only when an entrepreneur risks creating things from scratch with a dedicated and talented team to help bring ideas to fruition. Several studies have evidence of how critical people are as an asset to organisations (Popescu & Kyriakopoulos, 2022). Owner-managers of businesses must therefore learn to select, manage, and lead people to achieve the goals of their businesses for growth.

Another critical requirement for starting a business which should not be underestimated is the consideration of the sources of capital or funding for the business (Camilleri & Bresciani, 2022). Businesses may be started with equity, debt, or a combination of equity and debt. Sources of equity funding include personal savings, friends and relatives, venture capital, and angel investors. Sources of debt financing include friends and relatives, banks, and commercial finance companies,

3.3 Starting with the End Game in Mind

Entrepreneurs do not appear vague but have at least an idea of the end game of the business they want to create. The entrepreneurial path does not automatically result in the creation and possession of wealth as it is the process of idea transformation and customer acceptance of the products that ignites the latter process of wealth creation and distribution (Ali & Adegbe, 2019). As such, young entrepreneurs who are enthused about business creation and development should not focus and be overly excited about the results but rather on the learnings that come with the entrepreneurial nuggets of the process. This helps provide a road map and a shared learning experience both for the personal development of the entrepreneur and the human resources that are available or at the disposal of the former (Tittel & Terzidis, 2020). Having the endgame or goal in mind can be likened to a pilot flying a jet who has knowledge of the destination and applies the navigation and skills needed to direct the flight to the location. Having the endgame in mind does not guarantee that successful landing for an entrepreneur, but it assists in fine-tuning focus, capital, and human resource allocation as well as building strategic network and relationships that can steer the activities of the organisation or business (Cao & Shi, 2021).

3.4 Preparatory Stage for Starting a Business

3.4.1 Business Idea

Starting a business usually begins with having an idea that needs to be scrutinised critically to assess its merit and potential viability. The idea helps determine the specific product or service the business wishes to produce to meet the market demand or customer needs (Bauman & Lucy, 2021). A well appraised idea assists in the development of a business plan, which serves as a guiding document for the delivery of business activities and benchmarking targets against set goals. At the ideation stage, business starters need to read and learn more about the business they desire to venture into by talking to knowledgeable people, surfing the internet for relevant information, and finding mentors within the industry who would coach and guide them, while providing business insight and product market knowledge (Chavoushi et al., 2020). For some industries, having a unique product, a breakthrough invention, or a drastically new process right at the start of the business may not be a necessary element for most successful companies. For instance, in the computer industry, companies that thrive do not so often have their innovation or products accepted the first time but from the onset, most successful entrepreneurs are those who take advantage of small, uncertain opportunities, without necessarily having any breakthrough technology or invention (Liedtka, 2020). The most important thing is to start modestly on the back of a strong vision with a commitment to consistency and perseverance.

3.4.2 The Business and Vision

All great entrepreneurs have a vision about the kind of future they envisage for their product or service. They may never realise this from the beginning, but it is normal for them to alter some key elements as they progress, even trash some altogether, or for some, follow the vision successfully (El-Annan, 2013). Regardless of whatever happens with the vision, there must be evidence of its existence in the first place. Your vision is all about where you see what you have envisioned; a prognosis of the expression of what the "destination" would look like although sometimes the end of the beginning becomes the beginning of the end. For a typical entrepreneur, a business is like her child, born out of an idea. The hope of the entrepreneur is for that child to grow into a very valuable person as envisioned. A business grows as a result of its foreshadowed vision, skills, and the owner's drive, which is critical in propelling the business (Markman, Baron & Balkin, 2005). It is indeed the owner who first perceives the possibility of the business being formed and its subsequent growth. This makes the vision a very powerful glue that anchors and binds the business component together, without which the business will struggle to keep in shape (Antonakis & Autio, 2014).

3.4.3 Business Knowledge

When entrepreneurs hatch a business idea and get their vision sorted, the next thing is not for them to hire a consultant to prepare a business plan for them, as initial funds to do that may not be available. The next relevant move is to acquire relevant information about the business, particularly, the acquisition of market knowledge and know-how about market trends, key players, and existing competitive products. A professional could be hired to design a good survey to this effect, but otherwise, personal enquiry can be of significance here (González-Benito et al., 2009).

3.4.4 Business Plan

After going through the aforementioned, it is now time to write your business plan. When the idea has been crystallised into a product and the requisite market and industry knowledge has been acquired, the next step is to get a business plan prepared for the business (McKenzie, 2017). A business plan is a comprehensive well-thought-out predetermined course of action for the execution and operationalisation of a business (Abrams & Kleiner, 2003). A business plan comprises a document containing key information such as why the business was set up (mission); where the business hopes to be (vision); and the objectives, goals, and tactics of the business. It also discusses a market analysis and customer segmentation; outlines competitive landscape; and states the resources required to fund the business in the form of a financial plan while making financial projections for the business (Burns, 1996; Kahn & Baum, 2020). The product, pricing, promotion, and distribution policies as well as the framework of the business are also developed. Most importantly, the business plan outlines the supporting organisational structure and team formation or human resource needs to implement the plan (Bratton, Bratton & Steele, 2021). Again, a business plan serves as an "inverse" road map that helps an entrepreneur to develop how their vision will be fulfilled. It essentially works from the opposite direction as it presents the vision in the form of tangible elements. It fundamentally helps the business owner to capture every critical detail of the business serving as a blueprint to guide the business and to facilitate financing (Ranasinghe, 2021). A business plan takes its source and inspiration from the vision, using it as a benchmark, and out of which it develops its elements. It is best to conduct prior research to support the business plan with hard evidence where necessary to prevent some foreseeable mistakes. The one who develops and understands the business plan is even more important than the plan itself since most prospective investors will bet on the developer and not on your dreams.

3.5 Profile of an Entrepreneur

The personal attributes of an entrepreneur play a very useful role in the business start-up process (López-Núñez et al., 2020). An entrepreneur is perceived as someone with the determination to succeed and be his own boss. He is able to define or identify a unique opportunity or space within the market and this makes him an innovator (Chang & Chen, 2020). He also assumes an embodied risk–return connection, making him a calculated risk taker. The entrepreneur is also resourceful, in that he sets up and runs his business using available resources, coupled with his ability to connect products and people (Asante & Affum-Osei, 2019). The entrepreneur matches the opportunities that come with the challenges of the business with the requisite skills and translates them into a business activity. These attributes of the entrepreneur are essential to influence the success of a business (Salmony & Kanbach, 2022). While entrepreneurs are intelligent and may have remarkable marketing skills, what makes their businesses so successful is that their owners are extremely responsive and flexible. Their adaptability, personality, and willingness to provide expert products/services make all the difference and not the traditional industry expertise that they carry or rely on (Vodă & Florea, 2019). Entrepreneurs must also be versatile; have self-confidence and self-control; have a high desire for achievement; be action-oriented; and have a high tolerance for dynamic environment and human behaviour (Yasir et al., 2019).

Some growth entrepreneurs indicated that the following three components, building an awesome organisation, managing themselves, and funding businesses with high growth potential, were the most important factors to them as owners and managers. They did not mind delegating marketing, sales, product development, and services as well as hiring other people to monitor and alert them on changes in externalities to other people. However, they believed that their success or failure was critically and directly tied to how well they managed themselves as leaders and people in building a business that could sustain growth and their choice of financing options (Tittel & Terzidis, 2020). Other factors outlined to be responsible for the growth and success of businesses include giving attention to customers, managing employees, and good keeping records (Li et al., 2020). The relationship that exists between the attributes of the business owner and the firm's growth is perceived as critical for many reasons including most importantly, the business owners imprinting lasting impressions on their businesses which influence the behaviours and culture of these businesses (Hameed & Irfan, 2019).

3.5.1 Skills

Entrepreneurs require a skill set with regard to the managerial and technical aspects of the business. Essentially, both technical and soft business skills constitute the real-world skills and capabilities required to perform specific business-related tasks (Tittel & Terzidis, 2020). Managerial skills also cover hands-on knowledge of how to plan, organise, and manage both human and other resources as well as knowledge of associated regulations. Having the skill set is one important prerequisite to starting a business, and if an entrepreneur does not have it, he must acquire it through training, workshops, seminars, or through collaboration with someone with the needed skill set (Komarkova, Conrads & Collado, 2015). Owner-managers in a study in Kenya indicated that they formerly worked for organisations within the same industry that manufactured similar goods or services before starting their businesses and therefore understood the manufacturing processes and the markets alike; hence, the application of the experience and knowledge acquired to their businesses (Shimoli et al., 2020).

3.5.2 *Links and Contacts*

It is usual that the first few sales and marketing of a business are made through family, friends, work colleagues, and social clubs in order to build confidence to face total strangers as the sales network is developed (Chopra et al., 2021). By growing the business links in an entrepreneur's network of close associates, it facilitates trust building with business partners while nurturing other personality traits and functions of the business (Paul, 2019). The ensuing personal network of customers is then developed into a structural network of the business (Stephens, 2021).

3.6 Starting the Business

Once the preparatory stage is done, starting the business is next. This stage is the real deal and is very crucial. It requires careful thought and decision-making. More often, entrepreneurial ventures are prone to uncertain outcomes and extremely susceptible to falling flat immediately after kick-off or some months into the commencement of the business (Dvouletý & Orel, 2019). In many cases, entrepreneurial ventures are created in industries where there is a lack of a proven business model and no recognisable network of support. In order to ensure the development of a robust business, the following practices and components must be critically considered although this is not an exhaustive list.

3.6.1 *Choice of Forms of Business Ownership*

At this point, the entrepreneur has to decide which form of business owner-ship to employ in order to begin the business; whether to start afresh, buy an existing business, or acquire a franchise. Each of these has its own merits and demerits. Most people start their own businesses because it requires a relatively low initial capital in most cases as opposed to investing in a fran-chise operation or purchasing an existing business, which usually requires a significant capital investment. Other forms of business ownership including sole proprietorship, partnership, limited liability companies, corporations, and joint ventures have been afore-explained in Chapter 2.

3.6.2 *Bookkeeping Systems*

Bookkeeping is the recording and monitoring of a business's financial transactions. Bookkeepers regularly compile these activities into reports that illustrate the health of the business (Anheier & Seibel, 2022). Invoicing, paying bills, preparing tax returns, monitoring key performance indica-tors, and providing strategic advice may also be performed. Although some small business owners prefer to handle their own bookkeeping, they may encounter several obstacles if they lack the necessary knowledge (Aladejebi & Oladimeji, 2019). The benefits of bookkeeping lie in your ability to tell a numerical story of what is happening in your business, which can help you improve operations, increase profits, and avoid issues with local and federal tax agencies (Madurapperuma, Thilakerathne & Manawadu, 2016). In this way, thorough and accurate bookkeeping can help your business present its case to potential lenders and investors when seeking financ-ing. Bookkeeping enables businesses and its finances to be maintained and regulated in accordance with the law. Consequently, the benefits of book-keeping in businesses are tied to the insights provided by the numbers, which will help you determine what is going well and where there is room for improvement (Muchira, 2012).

3.6.3 *Developing and Choosing Your Team*

The people you work with are very crucial human resource elements for every business. They can make or the business. Hiring people and firing them when needed can be challenging especially when recruitments are not merit but relationship based (Meyer-Sahling et al., 2021). For start-ups, hiring an administrative staff will be an immediate need. Entrepreneurs must treat their staff as assets and not complements in the business process (Egeberg, Gornitzka & Trondal, 2019). Delegation is one of the means to achieve the best from the human resource of an organisation. Delegation of duties in business is critical as it creates opportunity for people development and providing people with challenges and new experiences as part of their in-house training (Ugoani, 2020). When delegating instructions must be clear in respect of what needs to be done, the degree of quality required, and the timelines set to achieve these set business targets.

3.6.4 Capital and Cash Flow Management

The growth of businesses demand capital and other resource investments. As the human resource increases, extra machinery and resources will also be needed including most importantly, working capital. Capital is one of the first critical requirements for every new business. The entrepreneur needs to find out how to acquire capital and explore different opportunities for financing through debt and equity (Muhammad et al., 2021). Cash flow management is how start-ups manage their sources of finances. Several businesses fail not for lack of innovative ideas or even the size of the cash flow but as a result of bad practices in cash flow management (Plaskova et al., 2020). The time lags between cash inflows and outflows could eventually affect business operations and overall output. As such, business owners should be mindful of account reconciliation practices where accounts payables and accounts receivables are given utmost attention (Kolias, Arnis & Karamanis, 2020).

3.6.5 Development of Customer Lists and Preferences

Entrepreneurs should develop a database of existing and potential customers, which comprises the name, contact details, and marketing approach to determine their preference for products and packages as well as services. This is termed as "customer segmentation" (Christy et al., 2021). Customer segmentation is an effective tool for businesses to closely align their strategy and tactics with, and better target, their current and future customers. Every customer is unique, as is every customer's journey; consequently, a single approach will rarely work for all. Customer segmentation helps to divide your customers up based on common characteristics – such as demographics or behaviours, so your marketing team or sales team can reach out to those customers more effectively (Sheikh, Ghanbarpour & Gholamiangonabadi, 2019). These customer segmentation groups may also serve as a starting point for discussions regarding the creation of marketing personas and product user personas. Effective customer segmentation analysis is typically used to inform a brand's messaging and positioning, helps organisations determine which new products and services they may wish to invest in, and reveals ways to improve the business's sales performance (Weinstein, 2020). In order for marketing personas to be effective, they must be closely aligned with these segments. Customer segmentation helps determine and understand customer needs better. A relationship approach should also be developed where a friendlier but professional style of exchange and conversation with customers is encouraged (Weinstein, 2012). In line with this, basic customer focus concepts and orientation of market segmentation, targeting, and positioning should be applied for smooth business operations.

3.7 Business Growth and Expansion

3.7.1 Relationships

Business relations are the connections that exist between all entities that engage in commerce. This includes the relationships between various stakeholders in a business network, such as those between employers and employees, employers and business partners, and all companies with which a business is affiliated (Hameed, Nisar & Wu, 2021). A company's business relations may include a long list of customers, vendors, sales leads, potential customers, banks, stockbrokers, the media, and service providers. Governmental agencies on the municipal, state, and federal levels can also be involved in business relations. Essentially, business relations are all of the individuals and entities with which a business is connected or expects to have a connection, whether internal or external. Businesses depend on the development and maintenance of vital relations with employees, business partners, suppliers, and customers – any person or entity that is involved in the business process (Alhathal, Sharma & Kingshott, 2019). Companies that intentionally cultivate and maintain connections may be more successful than those that ignore these connections. Strong business relations can promote customer awareness, customer retention, and collaboration between businesses in the supply chain. Hallmarks of good business relations include trust, loyalty, and communication (Cavaliere et al., 2021). Trust is essential to the success of long-term business relationships because it fosters employee satisfaction, cooperation, motivation, and creativity. Similarly, loyalty helps companies form strong and lasting relationships with employees, who return that loyalty by providing high-quality services (Larsson & Broström, 2020). That, in turn, can translate to high customer satisfaction and better sales because customers tend to pay more for products or services when they hold a company in high regard. Inherent to trust and loyalty is good communication, which is essential to managing and optimising internal and external business relations (Juanamasta et al., 2019). Establishing good communications protocols in the early stages of a company can facilitate and improve planning, projects, and policymaking. From a financial standpoint, business relations can often determine the success or failure of a company. While strong business relationships provide a competitive edge, weak relationships result in negative outcomes, including dissatisfied employees, customers, negative reputations, and limited growth (Manthiou, Hickman & Klaus, 2020).

3.7.2 *Growth and Expansion Options*

Increasing the capacity of an organisation in terms of machinery and production volumes is one option for growth and expansion. An organisation could also adopt strategies that make their customers extremely satisfied such that they direct all orders to them to the extent of attracting competitors' customers (Saraswati, 2022). Entrepreneurs in developing ventures could use the knowledge acquired previously from business transactions with suppliers and customers to develop an expansion plan. Diversification is another option companies can use to expand their businesses. Diversification could be done by introducing new products to an organisation's existing product range or modifying existing products (Omosa et al., 2022). Market diversification involves adding new clients to existing markets with existing product lines. Mergers and acquisitions as well as franchising could also be a considerable expansion (Hossain, 2021). The value-addition strategy for expansion is yet another. In particular, value-addition refers to the additional features a company may add to a product or service to increase its perceived value to customers or clients. Value-addition may involve modifying the product's design or adding extra accessories in order to increase the perceived value to consumers. Value-addition makes the product more valuable to the customers (Lavelli, 2021).

It is possible to combine any of these options for expansion. Some resource considerations in this growth and expansion process include new knowledge, additional capital, staff training, and new resources or connections. One other critical thing organisations should keep in mind is the development of systems to match the expansion; for instance, standardisation of work processes as well as benchmark development and systems for performance and operations (Soomro et al., 2021). A firm's business practices, growth-related attributes, and human resource practices also make a difference in its ability to achieve and maintain rapid growth. Additionally, firms that have made a real commitment to growth have a higher probability of achieving rapid growth than firms that have not made a comparable commitment (Herbane, 2019).

3.8 Conclusion

Starting and growing a business requires careful planning and decision-making, strategy implementation, knowledge, skill, creativity, agility, and tenacity. It requires a judiciously thought-out process implemented in stages to achieve the desired business results and goals. The key element for entrepreneurs is to pick what best suits their needs and customise them according to the dictates of the vision, mission, and objectives of the business. Possessing the desirable entrepreneurial attributes is also key in the successful setting up and growth of a business. The systems, great team selection and development, and financial management are equally critical. Business growth options vary and usually depend on the growth objective of the business, management decisions, strategic options, key business operations practices, commitment, focus, and available resources.

The COVID-19 pandemic has brought to the fore different sectors into which investors can invest. Areas such as pharmaceuticals and information technology come to mind. The method of doing business has seen great change and will continue to change with time. A lot of customers prefer using digital technology for most of their activities. Again, several internal operations and the management of the human resource within organisations are carried out using technology. Entrepreneurs should therefore take advantage to venture into areas which will address the needs of people and from which entrepreneurs will earn returns on their investments.

References

Abrams, R. M. & Kleiner, E. (2003). *The successful business plan: Secrets & strategies*. The Planning Shop.

Akter, B. & Iqbal, M. A. (2020). Failure factors of platform start-ups: A systematic literature review. *Nordic Journal of Media Management*, 1(3), 433–459.

Aladejebi, O. & Oladimeji, J. A. (2019). The impact of record keeping on the performance of selected small and medium enterprises in Lagos metropolis. *Journal of Small Business and Entrepreneurship Development*, 7(1), 28–40.

Alhathal, F. T., Sharma, P. & Kingshott, R. P. (2019). Moderating effects of service separation on customer relationships with service firms: A social-exchange perspective. *Journal of Service Theory and Practice*, 29(1), 71–92.

Ali, Y. & Adegbe, O. R. (2019). Effects of entrepreneurship engagements on white-collar jobs: A review of wealth creation in Nigeria. *Journal of Good Governance and Sustainable Development in Africa*, 5(1), 120–129.

Alpenidze, O., Pauceanu, A. M. & Sanyal, S. (2019). Key success factors for business incubators in Europe: An empirical study. *Academy of Entrepreneurship Journal*, 25(1), 1–13.

Anheier, H. K. & Seibel, H. D. (2022). Small-scale industries and economic development in Ghana: Business behavior and strategies in informal sector economies, 25(1), 1–13.

Antonakis, J. & Autio, E. (2014). Entrepreneurship and leadership. In: Robert, J. B., Michael, F., Robert, A. B. (eds) *The psychology of entrepreneurship* (pp. 221–240). Psychology Press, London.

Asante, E. A. & Affum-Osei, E. (2019). Entrepreneurship as a career choice: The impact of locus of control on aspiring entrepreneurs' opportunity recognition. *Journal of Business Research*, 98, 227–235.

Asongu, S. A. & Odhiambo, N. M. (2019). Challenges of doing business in Africa: A systematic review. *Journal of African Business*, 20(2), 259–268.

Bauman, A. & Lucy, C. (2021). Enhancing entrepreneurial education: Developing competencies for success. *The International Journal of Management Education*, 19(1), 100293.

Bratton, J., Gold, J., Bratton, A. & Steele, L. (2021). *Human resource management*. Bloomsbury Publishing.

Burns, P. (1996). The business plan. In: Burns, P., Dewhurst, J. (eds) *Small business and entrepreneurship* (pp. 180–197). Palgrave, London.

Camilleri, M. A. & Bresciani, S. (2022). Crowdfunding small businesses and start-ups: A systematic review, an appraisal of theoretical insights and future research directions. *European Journal of Innovation Management*. https://doi.org/10.1108/EJIM-02-2022-0060.

Cao, Z. & Shi, X. (2021). A systematic literature review of entrepreneurial ecosystems in advanced and emerging economies. *Small Business Economics*, 57(1), 75–110.

Cavaliere, L. P. L., Khan, R., Rajest, S. S., Sundram, S., Jainani, D. K., Bagale, D. G., Chakravarthi, M. K. & Regin, R. (2021). The impact of customer relationship management on customer satisfaction and retention: The mediation of service quality. *Turkish Journal of Physiotherapy and Rehabilitation*, 32(3), 22107–22121.

Chang, Y. Y. & Chen, M. H. (2020). Creative entrepreneurs' creativity, opportunity recognition, and career success: Is resource availability a double-edged sword? *European Management Journal*, 38(5), 750–762.

Chavoushi, Z. H., Nicholls-Nixon, C. L. & Valliere, D. (2020). Mentoring fit, social learning, and venture progress during business incubation. *The Journal of Applied Business and Economics*, 22(14), 23–39.

Chopra, A., Avhad, V. & Jaju, A. S. (2021). Influencer marketing: An exploratory study to identify antecedents of consumer behavior of millennial. *Business Perspectives and Research*, 9(1), 77–91.

Christy, A. J., Umamakeswari, A., Priyatharsini, L. & Neyaa, A. (2021). RFM ranking–An effective approach to customer segmentation. *Journal of King Saud University – Computer and Information Sciences*, 33(10), 1251–1257.

Dvouletý, O. & Orel, M. (2019). Entrepreneurial activity and its determinants: Findings from African developing countries. In: Ratten, V., Jones, P., Braga, V., Marques, C.S. (eds) *Sustainable entrepreneurship: The role of collaboration in the global economy* (pp. 9–24). Springer, Cham.

Egeberg, M., Gornitzka, Å. & Trondal, J. (2019). Merit-based recruitment boosts good governance: How do European Union agencies recruit their personnel? *International Review of Administrative Sciences*, 85(2), 247–263.

El-Annan, S. H. (2013). Innovation, proactive, and vision are three integrated dimensions between leadership and entrepreneurship. *European Journal of Business and Social Sciences*, 1(12), 148–163.

González-Benito, Ó., González-Benito, J. & Muñoz-Gallego, P. A. (2009). Role of entrepreneurship and market orientation in firms' success. *European Journal of Marketing*, 43(3/4), 500–522.

Hameed, I. & Irfan, Z. (2019). Entrepreneurship education: A review of challenges, characteristics and opportunities. *Entrepreneurship Education*, 2(3–4), 135–148.

Hameed, W. U., Nisar, Q. A. & Wu, H. C. (2021). Relationships between external knowledge, internal innovation, firms' open innovation performance, service innovation and business performance in the Pakistani hotel industry. *International Journal of Hospitality Management*, 92, 102745.

Herbane, B. (2019). Rethinking organizational resilience and strategic renewal in SMEs. *Entrepreneurship and Regional Development*, 31(5–6), 476–495.

Hossain, M. S. (2021). Merger & Acquisitions (M&As) as an important strategic vehicle in business: Thematic areas, research avenues & possible suggestions. *Journal of Economics and Business*, 116, 106004.

Hossinger, S. M., Chen, X. & Werner, A. (2020). Drivers, barriers and success factors of academic spin-offs: A systematic literature review. *Management Review Quarterly*, 70(1), 97–134.

Juanamasta, I. G., Wati, N. M. N., Hendrawati, E., Wahyuni, W., Pramudianti, M., Wisnujati, N. S., Setiawati, A. P., Susetyorini, S., Elan, U., Rusdiyanto, R. & Astanto, D. (2019). The role of customer service through customer relationship management (CRM) to increase customer loyalty and good image. *International Journal of Scientific and Technology Research*, 8(10), 2004–2007.

Kahn, M. J. & Baum, N. (2020). Entrepreneurship and formulating business plans. In: Baum, N., Kahn, M. (eds) *The business basics of building and managing a healthcare practice* (pp. 37–41). Springer, Cham.

Kim, Y. K. & Sullivan, P. (2019). Emotional branding speaks to consumers' heart: The case of fashion brands. *Fashion and Textiles*, 6(1), 1–16.

Kolias, G., Arnis, N. & Karamanis, K. (2020). The simultaneous determination of cash conversion cycle components. *Accounting and Management Information Systems*, 19(2), 311–332.

Komarkova, I., Conrads, J. & Collado, A. (2015). Entrepreneurship competence: An overview of existing concepts. Policies and initiatives. Depth case study report. (JRC96531).

Larsson, A. & Broström, E. (2020). Ensuring customer retention: Insurers' perception of customer loyalty. *Marketing Intelligence and Planning*, 38(2), 151–166.

Lavelli, V. (2021). Circular food supply chains–Impact on value addition and safety. *Trends in Food Science and Technology*, 114, 323–332.

Li, C., Murad, M., Shahzad, F., Khan, M. A. S., Ashraf, S. F. & Dogbe, C. S. K. (2020). Entrepreneurial passion to entrepreneurial behavior: Role of entrepreneurial alertness, entrepreneurial self-efficacy and proactive personality. *Frontiers in Psychology*, 11, 1611.

Liedtka, J. (2020). Putting technology in its place: Design thinking's social technology at work. *California Management Review*, 62(2), 53–83.

López-Núñez, M. I., Rubio-Valdehita, S., Aparicio-García, M. E. & Díaz-Ramiro, E. M. (2020). Are entrepreneurs born or made? The influence of personality. *Personality and Individual Differences*, 154, 109699.

Madurapperuma, M. W., Thilakerathne, P. M. C. & Manawadu, I. N. (2016). Accounting record keeping practices in small and medium sized enterprise's (SME's) in Sri Lanka. *Journal of Finance and Accounting*, 4(4), 188–193.

Mahaputra, M. R. (2021). Relationship word of mouth, advertising and product quality to brand awareness. *Dinasti International Journal of Digital Business Management*, 2(6), 1099–1108.

Manthiou, A., Hickman, E. & Klaus, P. (2020). Beyond good and bad: Challenging the suggested role of emotions in customer experience (CX) research. *Journal of Retailing and Consumer Services*, 57, 102218.

Markman, G. D., Baron, R. A. & Balkin, D. B. (2005). Are perseverance and self-efficacy costless? Assessing entrepreneurs' regretful thinking. *Journal of Organizational Behavior: The International Journal of Industrial Occupational and Organizational Psychology and Behavior*, 26(1), 1–19.

McKenzie, D. (2017). Identifying and spurring high-growth entrepreneurship: Experimental evidence from a business plan competition. *American Economic Review*, 107(8), 2278–2307.

Meyer-Sahling, J., Mikkelsen, K. S. & Schuster, C. (2021). Merit recruitment, tenure protections and public service motivation: Evidence from a conjoint experiment with 7,300 public servants in Latin America, Africa and Eastern Europe. *Public Administration*, 99(4), 740–757.

Muchira, B. W. (2012). Record keeping and growth of micro and small enterprises: A case study of Thika municipality in Kenya. Retrieved on 15-11-16.

Muhammad, M., Ei Yet, C., Tahir, M. & Nasir, A. M. (2021). Capital structure of family firms: The effect of debt and equity market timing. *Journal of Family Business Management*, 11(1), 1–18.

Omosa, H. M., Muya, J., Omari, S. & Momanyi, C. (2022). Role of product diversification strategy on performance of selected tea factories in Kenya. *International Academic Journal of Innovation, Leadership and Entrepreneurship*, 2(2), 279–296.

Paul, J. (2019). Marketing in emerging markets: A review, theoretical synthesis and extension. *International Journal of Emerging Markets*, 15(3), 446–468.

Plaskova, N. S., Prodanova, N. A., Ignatyeva, O. V., Nayanov, E. A., Goncharov, V. V. & Surpkelova, A. (2020). Controlling in cash flow management of the company. *Eurasian Journal of Biosciences*, 14(2), 3507–3512.

Popescu, C. R. G. & Kyriakopoulos, G. L. (2022). Strategic human resource management in the 21st-century organizational landscape: Human and intellectual capital as drivers for performance management. In: Cristina, R. G. P (ed.) *COVID-19 pandemic impact on new economy development and societal change* (pp. 296–323). IGI Global.

Ranasinghe, H. K. G. S. (2021). Business planning practices affecting higher level of business performance of manufacturing SMEs in the western province of Sri Lanka. *International Journal of Social Relevance & Concern*, 9(7), 237–260.

Salamzadeh, A. & Kirby, D. A. (2017). New venture creation: How start-ups grow? *AD-Minister*, No. 30, Medellin, January–June, 9–29.

Salmony, F. U. & Kanbach, D. K. (2022). Personality trait differences across types of entrepreneurs: A systematic literature review. *Review of Managerial Science*, 16(3), 713–749.

Saraswati, E. (2022). Market orientation, service quality on customer satisfaction and loyalty: Study on sharia banking in Indonesia. *Golden Ratio of Marketing and Applied Psychology of Business*, 2(1), 26–41.

Sheikh, A., Ghanbarpour, T. & Gholamiangonabadi, D. (2019). A preliminary study of fintech industry: A two-stage clustering analysis for customer segmentation in the B2B setting. *Journal of Business-to-Business Marketing*, 26(2), 197–207.

Shimoli, S. M., Cai, W., Abbas Naqvi, M. H. & Lang, Q. (2020). Entrepreneurship success traits. Do Kenyans possess the desired entrepreneur personality traits for enhanced e-entrepreneurship? Case study of Kenyan students in the People's Republic of China. *Cogent Business & Management*, 7(1), 1847863.

Soomro, B. A., Mangi, S. & Shah, N. (2021). Strategic factors and significance of organizational innovation and organizational learning in organizational performance. *European Journal of Innovation Management*, 24(2), 481–506.

Stephens, S. (2021). Building an entrepreneurial network: The experience of business graduates. *Journal of Entrepreneurship Education*, 24(1), 1–13.

Tittel, A. & Terzidis, O. (2020). Entrepreneurial competences revised: Developing a consolidated and categorized list of entrepreneurial competences. *Entrepreneurship Education*, 3(1), 1–35.

Ugoani, J. (2020). Effective delegation and its impact on employee performance. *International Journal of Economics and Business Administration*, 6(3), 78–87.

Venesz, B., Dőry, T. & Raišienė, A. G. (2022). Characteristics of lead users in different stages of the new product development process: A systematic review in the context of open innovation. *Journal of Open Innovation: Technology, Market, and Complexity*, 8(1), 24.

Vodă, A. I. & Florea, N. (2019). Impact of personality traits and entrepreneurship education on entrepreneurial intentions of business and engineering students. *Sustainability*, 11(4), 1192.

Weinstein, A. (2012). *Superior customer value: Strategies for winning and retaining customers*. CRC Press.

Weinstein, A. (2020). Creating superior customer value in the now economy. *Journal of Creating Value*, 6(1), 20–33.

Yasir, N., Liren, A., Mehmood, N. & Arfat, Y. (2019). Impact of personality traits on entrepreneurial intention and demographic factors as moderator. *International Journal of Entrepreneurship*, 23(1), 1–20.

Chapter Questions

1. Clearly describe the steps associated with forming a business.
2. Describe the business growth process.
3. Explain the benefits and challenges associated with entrepreneurship.
4. Critically examine the statement that the success of a business lies in the process and not the results.
5. Describe the personal entrepreneurial attributes essential to a business success.
6. Describe the skill set required by every entrepreneur to run a business successfully.
7. What is the importance of bookkeeping in a new business?

Chapter 4

The Management Functions

Learning Outcomes

After completing this chapter, you should be able to:

- explain the concept of planning and the phases of the planning process.
- describe organisational objectives and policies.
- explain forecasting and how it relates to business.
- explain SWOT analysis model and TOWS matrix.
- describe organisational decision-making process.
- explain the concept of organising and the basic forms of organisational structures.
- describe a bureaucratic organisation and its merits and demerits.
- explain the types of leadership styles and its associated theories and motivations.
- explain the concept of controlling and the tools applied.

Chapter Outline

- Introduction
- Planning
- Policies and Procedures
- Forecasting
- Decision-Making

DOI: 10.4324/9781003458524-4

- Organising
- Staffing
- Directing
- Controlling
- Conclusion
- References
- Case Study
- Sources

4.1 Introduction

Every business seeks to achieve the goals it sets for itself within stipulated periods. The role of the manager is to ensure that the inputs (resources or capabilities) available to the organisation are transformed into achieving these desired goals. The sequences of activities that managers employ in effectively performing their roles are what we refer to fundamentally as management functions. Thus, the management function is a social process involving the duty for the efficient and cost-effective planning and regulatory oversight of an enterprise's operations in order to achieve specified goals. Management function is a dynamic process comprising numerous components and actions. It is important to note that these functions need to be performed sequentially since managers cannot direct the activities of their employees if the necessary planning has not been considered and executed. The fundamental functions involved in the management process include planning, organising, staffing, directing, and controlling (Hales, 2019; Cagle et al., 2020).

4.2 Planning

This chapter explains planning as a fundamental and an inevitable managerial function. It explores the different phases of the planning process while identifying the key activities that managers perform at each stage to effectively transform the business''s resources into desired outputs (Păunescu & Argatu, 2020). Of the five fundamental functions of management, planning is the prime as it commences the process of management. The basic function of planning is to determine an 'organisation's desirable goals and then decide on the strategies to adopt to achieve those goals. Planning calls for

managers to be aware of the varying environmental conditions their organisation is faced with and subsequently predict conditions for the future
(Longva, Strand & Pasquine, 2020) and also exhibit the ability to make good
decisions.

All managers engage in different forms of planning. The kind of planning that a manager engages in is dependent on his level of authority in the
organisation. Top managers make plans and take decisions with the overall
direction of the organisation in mind, whereas managers responsible for
the various divisions in the organisation make plans and take decisions that
seek to further the set goals of their sections while staying within the framework of the 'organisation's goal as a whole (Kahn & Baum, 2020). Managers
employ several resources in the planning process intending to transform
these inputs into outputs. The resources that managers employ include the
following:

Inputs	Transformation	Output
Human, financial, physical, information, and entrepreneurship resources	a. Physical transformation process b. Management process	a. Achievement of goals b. Products c. Services d. Productivity e. Job creation f. Profit

Source: Authors' created table (2023)

4.2.1 The Planning Process

The planning process includes five stages, and every good manager is
expected to follow these stages to develop plans that will result in the realisation of the goals of the organisation. The five stages are as follows: establishing objectives, developing premises, decision-making, implementing a
course of action, and monitoring and evaluating results.

a. Establishing objectives: To begin the planning process, objectives and
   goals are set by the organisation. This helps managers identify and
   communicate the sense of direction of the organisation''s efforts and
   similarly direct the focus of the organisation on the expected results.
   For the activities to be very effective, the stated objectives should be

clear, specific, and written in explicit language for comprehension by all and sundry involved in the organisation (Jauhiainen, 2019). In this vein, objectives should be workable, hands-on, acceptable by all, and attainable.

b. Developing premises: Premises facilitate the description of future scenarios to provide a framework for identifying, evaluating, and selecting a course of action. They serve as a basis for planning. Developing premises means making assumptions or forecasts of the future taking into consideration conditions that could affect the operations of the organisation. The forecast or the assumptions about the future which provide a basis for planning in the present are also referred to as planning premises. Planning premises may be internal or external (Honig & Samuelsson, 2021). Internal premises can be controlled or within the control remit of the organisation, whereas external premises cannot be controlled.

c. Decision-making: Decision-making can be described as purposely selecting the action to take from a set of alternatives to achieve organisational or managerial objectives or goals (Zhang et al., 2021). The decision-making process is a continuous and indispensable element of managing any business activities. After the necessary premises are established, several alternative courses of action have to be considered. Each alternative should be evaluated through a comparison of its pros and cons while taking into consideration the resources available and the requirements of the organisation. After considering these alternatives, the best course of action is then taken.

d. Implementing a course of action: The next phase of the planning process is the implementation phase. Management must provide detailed instructions that cover individuals responsible for specific activities and resources to be allocated to the plan (Nekhaychuk et al., 2019. Implementation is considered by some to be one of the critical execution keys to effective planning. Without proper implementation, a plan is nothing more than a mere wish.

e. Monitoring and evaluating results: Once a chosen plan is executed, it is imperative to measure whether it has been effective or not (. This can best be done using feedback or information received from departments or persons concerned. Monitoring enables the management to correct deviations or modify the plan as best fit. The final step of the planning process is the evaluation phase. Managers must continually assess how successful their plans have been and take remedial action as soon as it becomes necessary.

4.3 Objectives

1. Business objectives are the measurable, specific outcomes that companies hope to sustain as their organisations expand. When developing a list of business objectives, you focus on the particulars. Focusing on the particulars involves analysing, evaluating, and comprehending your current situation and future goals. The business objectives are its driving force. The business objective is a future destination the company hopes to reach. The purpose for which a business is established and carried out is its objective (Fairlie & Fossen, 2020). In every area where performance and outcomes directly affect the survival and prosperity of a business, objectives are required. The proper selection of objectives is crucial to the success of a business as objectives are expressed as statements of what needs to be accomplished within set timelines. Managers are required to establish objectives as part of the planning process, together with alternative activities geared at achieving the objectives. After a careful evaluation of the alternatives, managers must decide on the best course of action and take the necessary steps to ensure that the selected plans are effectively implemented (Fischer et al., 2020). Broadly, objectives can be viewed from an economic and social lens.

4.3.1 Economic Objectives

These objectives are directly linked to the inputs and returns aimed at the survival and performance of the company for both the short- and long-term sustenance of business. They include critical areas such as maximisation of profit and shareholders'' wealth, customer creation and market share, and productivity. These three areas are summarised as the triangular economic objective of the business.

■ *Maximisation of profit and shareholders'' wealth*: A business is a collection of activities pursued with the intention of generating a profit. Profit is the excess of revenue over expenditures. Profitability is the primary objective of any enterprise without which the business may not survive. Profit is essential for the growth and expansion of a business. Profits ensure a steady flow of capital for future business modernisation and expansion. Profits also indicate the level of business organisation'''s stability, productivity, and development. It is in the light of these that shareholders" investments are maximised to retain existing and winning potential investors into the business (O'Connell & Ward, 2020).

■ *Customer creation and market share:* Before the conversation and achievement of profits for any business enterprise, one of the cardinal and integral stakeholders in the equation are customers. Customers, whether individuals or businesses (like B2B), determine the sales level, and this makes the place of customers in the business equation very inevitable as their purchasing power is what keeps the business moving, thus ensuring the long-term sustenance of the enterprise (Hu et al., 2019). The business's long-term viability is entirely dependent upon its market share. The market share of the business is key to profit forecasting and budgeting. The business's primary purpose is the production of goods and the fulfilment of customer requirements (Tuominen et al., 2022). In order to increase demand and for that matter profit, the business must provide products of superior quality and value.

■ *Productivity:* Productivity is a metric for measuring the effectiveness of business operations. To ensure its survival and growth, every business must strive for higher levels of productivity (Van den Bosch & Vanormelingen, 2023). The use of innovation and employment of the right workforce will result in higher levels of productivity which will, other things being equal, lead to increased revenues.

4.3.2 Social Objectives

The purpose of business is to serve society, not just to generate profits and maximise shareholders wealth alone. The business sector is one of the societal pillars that serves a critical function in the development of society as the flourishing of a business is heavily dependent on the utilisation of the resources of the society. Some of the social objectives of a business include provision of goods and services, employment generation, and community impact. These triangular functions of business to society are key in fostering the social wealth of societies.

■ *Provision of goods and services:* The primary purpose of business is to satisfy the needs, demands, and wants of society (Tomashevska & Hryhoruk, 2022). Provision of goods and services is the prime social objective of the business. Products and services should be of higher quality and made available at reasonable prices which can be afforded by all and sundry, especially to those who are vulnerable and are in lower income bracket. As part of the social responsibility, businesses are to avoid misdeeds that may jeopardise the lives and properties of the people they serve. Corporate social responsibility will be discussed in detail in Chapter 8.

■ *Employment generation:* Unemployment from time immemorial is a significant issue that has threatened the economic and social fibre of countries globally and is also a canker facing the current generation (Donkor, 2021). Business generates employment, which essentially provides economic opportunities for people. Consequently, the social purpose of a business is to provide opportunities for advantageous employment to members of society while offering competitive remuneration and compensation packages.

■ *Community impact:* Contribution of businesses to society is captured as the corporate social responsibility of organisations (Tiba et al., 2019). Businesses create foundations and partner with non-governmental organisations to create impact projects which contribute to the advancement of society. Companies construct schools, colleges, libraries, hospitals, sports organisations, and research institutions through social philanthropy.

Some advantages of carefully thought-out objectives include the following:

1. Encapsulating the main ideas and theories relating to what the firm hopes to achieve or accomplish in the long run.
2. Serving as the basis for directing and guiding the organisation and also setting targets which allow the efforts of individual workers, units, and departments to be properly monitored and assisted where necessary.
3. Providing a sense of unity to the various divisions or groups within the organisation and also serving as motivation to everyone. This is because individuals realise how their individual contributions are integrated into the overall organisational goals.

4.4 Policies and Procedures

The company's policies and procedures are a set of internal guidelines that establish the company's rules and expectations. Policies and procedures assist in conveying to employees what they can and cannot do, as well as how they should behave. Policies are the framework for the company's rules and regulations. They establish guidelines for the management of potential issues and align the vision and values of an organisation with its daily operations (Tharanya et al., 2022). Examples of company policies include those pertaining to employee conduct, dress code, attendance, equal opportunity, and other aspects of employment terms and conditions. Each policy created should include a statement of its purpose, an explanation of why it was developed, a list of those to whom the policy applies, a description of acceptable and unacceptable behaviour, and the consequences for non-compliance (Li et al., 2019). Procedures are the means by which employees should respond to potential violations of company policies. For example, how they should report discrimination if they witness it. Policies, whether written or unwritten, serve as a guide in making decisions in a particular organisation. Policy decisions are the responsibility of top management, specifically the chief executive officer or the Board. Managers should involve subordinates in the policy-making process (Rehman, Mohamed & Ayoup, 2019). As mentioned before, policies do not always come in the form of writing as they can also be formulated by way of an oral understanding. However, they should be clear, understandable, observable, and stable. Once these qualities are present, the policies can now serve their purpose properly.

Advantages of policies and procedures include the following:

1. They serve as precedents to save time in the decision-making process.
2. They help managers achieve coordination.
3. Allow managers to delegate authority confidently.
4. Serve as templates or guides to actions when decisions are to be taken. This helps in making quick and accurate decisions.
5. Allow for more decisions to be taken at the lower levels of the organisational hierarchy.
6. Provide a blanket framework that stems from a summary of past experiences; this helps speed up the decision-making process.

4.4.1 Types of Policies

1. Originated policies: Every organisation aims at attaining a set of predetermined objectives. Originated policies are formulated by members of the top-level management. These policies have the primary aim of guiding and directing the actions of subordinates. Some top-level managers actively consult lower level managers in deciding on these policies.

2. Implied policies: Some policies evolve by themselves after managers take a series of decisions over some time. These policies do not exist in written form and are not formulated through a conscious process, but these policies emerge or evolve from managerial decisions of a recurring nature.

3. Appealed policies: These are made or formulated by managers at the top level, usually in response to appeals that managers at a lower level make. Appealed policies also exist as precedents to serve as guidelines for future decisions.

4. Externally imposed policies: Externally imposed policies stem not from the decisions or actions of managers but are influenced by the policies of external bodies such as the government, trade unions, trade associations, and other public agencies.

4.5 Forecasting

The future has always been uncertain and filled with many different possibilities. It is therefore important for managers to make calculated predictions when planning. This allows plans to stand the test of time and makes it easier to deal with unforeseen circumstances. Economic forecasting is a fundamental element of the planning process (Khan et al., 2020). Economic forecasting comes before the preparation of budgets and is mainly concerned with future probabilities. Sales forecasts are made considering various factors such as general economic, industrial, political, and international trends as well as trends relating to competitors" strengths and manufacturing costs (Ma & Fildes, 2021). Other factors affecting forecasting include the location where the business is situated, living and price levels, population trends, government controls and fiscal policies, and the technical environment as well as employment, productivity, and national income.

Forecasts also help in generating premises, from which managers can develop plans and select the right objectives. Forecasts are also very important because they cause managers to think into the future and plan accordingly.

■ *Limitations of forecasting*
   a. Past data reliability: Previous events are often evaluated to serve as a reference for the future. The problem, however, relates to how accurately these past events were recorded.

b. Accuracy of judgment: This is necessary to derive accurate factors which will influence the forecast, deduce interpretations from the data, and choose the evaluation methods to be applied to the emerging circumstances and challenges.

c. Measurement: Measuring forecasts must be done with a consistent base as single-base forecasts may not produce satisfactory results.

■ *Methods involved in forecasting*

Forecasting is done using a variety of approaches depending on factors such as the kind of information available and the type of product for which the forecast is being done for. Forecasting methods may range from extrapolating trends of technology or patterns that have developed over a while to more qualitative methods such as the Delphi technique.

■ *Position or situation analysis*

It is always important to have a system that allows regular y analysis of firm"s external environment to develop a strategic position (Cao & Chen, 2019). Such a system could be made up of the following:

1. Examining the environment to determine what factors are affecting the organisation and then conduct further assessment of these influences.

2. Assessing the key environmental factors and how relevant they are to the business. This means examining
   i. Barriers to entry for new firms (Mondliwa, 2020)
   ii. Level of competition in the industry (Distanont & Khongmalai, 2020)
   iii. Strength and nature of substitutes (Tsao et al., 2019)
   iv. The amount of power held by buyers (Gilboa & Mitchell, 2020)
   v. The amount of power held by suppliers (Ponte, 2019)

3. Identify the competitive position of the business. This can be done by mapping out the power of competitors by looking at the shares they each hold in certain segments of the market.

4. After assessing the organisation"s external environment, what comes next is to conduct an assessment of the business" resources based on information about its strengths and weaknesses (Namugenyi et al., 2019). Analysing and assessing the main resources of a firm help to form a background for judging the firm as a whole and assessing its effectiveness and efficiency. It is important to include its planning and control systems, organisational structure and its effectiveness, and the operating procedures of the firm.

5. For the organisation"s strengths and weaknesses to be examined, one can consider the firm"s present strategies and whether they can deal with all the changes happening in the business environment. Some common methods that can be used for such appraisals are as follows:

   a. SWOT analysis – The acronym SWOT represents the Strengths, Weaknesses, Opportunities, and Threats. This analytical method tries to match the internal strengths and weaknesses of the organisation against the opportunities and threats that are discovered through an analysis of both the internal and external environments (Benzaghta et al., 2021). This is a popular and simple method whose goal is to relate the identified opportunities and threats against the strengths of the organisation. It only aims at providing some rating of the identifiable opportunities and threats and how the current strategies of the organisation address the issue of the changing environment.

   b. TOWS matrix – The acronym TOWS represents Threats, Opportunities, Weakessness and Strengths. The TOWS matrix is another framework of analysis that allows the organisation to match its strengths and weaknesses with external opportunities and threats. TOWS is a variation of SWOT and was developed by Heinz Weirich, an American international professor of business (Dewanto, 2022). He derived the TOWS matrix from the SWOT analysis model. The TOWS matrix aims at identifying strategic options from an external-internal analysis and is relatively more practice-oriented, particularly in marketing and business administration fields. While SWOT analysis begins with an analysis of the internal environment consisting of the organisation"s strengths and weaknesses, the TOWS matrix begins with the external analysis first, followed by the internal.

4.6 Decision-Making

Decision-making forms an essential part of contemporary management functions. Managers make countless decisions daily consciously or otherwise legitimising their role as a critical element in the delivery of their managerial duties. Management decisions shape organisational activities and are essentially a continuous process. A decision is usually a specific action selected from alternative decisions in achieving the organisation and management objectives and for organisational productivity and sustenance (Weygandt, Kimmel & Aly, 2020).

4.6.1 Types of Decisions in Organisations

The key types of organisational decisions are outlined as follows:

Programmed decisions: These decisions are usually made by managers at the lower level in respect of routine or in response to repetitive challenges. They adopt standard procedures already established for managing such peculiar challenges. Programmed decisions are applied to issues such as raw material purchases, the supply of goods to a customer, the provision of implements, and employees" leave.

Non-programmed decisions: These high-level decisions relate to situations that are of great importance to the organisation and for which there is no straightforward solution. These include new product introduction to the market, opening new branches, and dealing with the absenteeism of a large number of employees and strike actions.

Routine and strategic decisions: These refer to the operational decisions of an organisation and require little or no assessment and analysis. Routine decisions are made often and can be taken quickly, subject to organisational policy. As such, lower level members within the organisation are allowed to take such decisions in light of the organisation"s policy framework. However, decisions of strategic nature are of relatively greater importance and are taken by high-level management as they impact organisational policy and objectives. These decisions are usually not repeated and can only be made after careful consideration of alternatives such as issues involving huge funds or investments or funds (Hauser, Eggers & Güldenberg, 2020).

Tactical (policy) and operational decisions: Policy decisions are about several organisational policy issues. These are decisions made by top-level management and usually have a long-term influence on the operations of the organisation (Fuertes et al., 2020). These include decisions on production volumes, distribution channels, and plant location, among others. On the other hand, operational decisions border on the day-to-day running of the business and are made by lower level and middle-level managers.

Major and minor decisions: Decisions made in organisations are also classified as major and minor. For instance, decisions relating to the acquisition of new buildings to serve as the organisation"s factory are a major one. Major decisions are very important and are therefore taken by top management. A simpler decision, such as the procurement of stationery for the office, constitutes a minor decision which could be made by an officer.

Committee decisions: Decisions may be made collectively by selected individuals such as standing committees on boards. These committees are used for largely very relevant organisational matters and constitute the main aim in taking group decisions to involve a maximum number of people in the decision-making process.

4.6.2 *The Decision-Making Process*

Decision-making is one of the most vital aspects of any organisation, whether a small business or a large one, and as such to get the best results, the process used to arrive at a decision must be rigorous and robust. Inasmuch as the executive body or the top-level management team will take the major decisions, there are some other decisions that lower level managers, supervisors, and other staff members will have to take, sometimes without input from their superiors. To ensure that there is a high level of uniformity in decision-making throughout an organisation, executives must implement a process that everyone can follow.

Organising as a management function comprises the development of an organogram and assigning the necessary resources to facilitate the achievement of the organisational objectives. The organisational structure serves as a framework and plays an important function in ensuring the coordination of individual and departmental efforts. The organisational structure is usually represented graphically in the form of an organisation chart and outlines the lines of authority within the organisation (surf the internet for several templates) (Phair & King, 1998; Van Looy, 2020). Organising also plays a role in the designing of individual jobs. These decisions concerning individual jobs are taken note of to outline the duties and responsibilities of each person as well as how workers are expected to carry out their duties. These decisions that concern themselves primarily with the nature of individual jobs in the company are generally referred to as "job design" decisions (Rios et al., 2020).

Organising at the management level involves decisions on assemblage of jobs into departments to ensure effective coordination of individual efforts. Departmentalising can be done in many different ways, some of which are organised by function, customer needs, product target, or by geographical considerations (Islami et al., 2021). The size of the organisation may impact the variety of methods managers would use in determining the size of their departments. Organising at the job level involves the designing of individual roles to make the maximum and most effective use of the company"s human resources.

Job design for instance was traditionally dependent on the principles of division of labour and specialisation. This was based on the assumption that individuals become more proficient in performing a job when the job content is relatively narrower. Experience has proven, however, that the possibility of a job becoming too narrow and specialised still exists, and when this happens, it could lead to decreased job satisfaction and commitment of individuals, which could also lead to increased absenteeism and turnover, among other negative outcomes. In today"s world, many companies have recently made efforts to strike the balance between the essential need for individuals to be specialised in their jobs and the need for them to perform jobs characterised by variety and autonomy (Schouten, 2019). Consequently, many managers design jobs based on principles such as job enrichment and teamwork. Managers need to realise that for any of the business"s goals to be attained, individual jobs must be logically grouped and the necessary authority be granted to prevent disagreements or conflict (Verma, Lamsal & Verma, 2022).

4.7 Organising

Organising is the process of integrating physical, financial, and human resources and developing productive relationships between them in order to achieve organisational objectives. To organise a business is to provide it with all the resources necessary for its operation, including raw materials, equipment, capital, and personnel (Ramakrishna, 2019). To organise a business requires determining and providing the organisational structure with human and non-human resources. Identification of activities, classification of groupings of activities, assignment of duties, delegation of authority and creation of responsibility, and coordination of authority and responsibility relationships comprise the organising process.

4.7.1 Principles of Organisation

1. Principle of unity of objectives: Unity of objectives in an organisation is necessary. The overall goals that the organisation seeks to achieve, the departmental goals, and the goals that each individual is assigned must

all be clearly defined. Desired goals cannot be properly achieved when there is a contradiction among the different levels of goals in the organisation. All these goals and objectives must be uniform.

2. Principle of specialisation: This principle usually relates to employees and workers. The term specialisation comes into play when an employee acquires a special type of knowledge and skill in any area. Specialisation helps organisations attain efficiency; it is, therefore, a necessity of all modern business organisations.

3. Principle of coordination: Organisations make use of many different equipment and tools; coordination is what helps organisations make the most of group effort and ensure unity of action.

4. Principle of authority: Authority generally flows from the top management to the lower management. It is the power or right that a person is accorded through which he can guide and direct the actions of others in achieving organisational goals. Authority is not necessarily vested in an individual, but in the position that the person occupies, and as such once he or she vacates the position, he leaves the authority behind. Authority is also important when it comes to decision-making and delegation of duty.

5. Principle of delegation: Delegation is simply referred to as the process by which a manager or someone in a high position transfers authority while creating responsibility for a subordinate to perform or accomplish a certain task. The authority delegated should be sufficient to allow the individual to carry out the responsibility that is assigned to the individual.

6. Principle of efficiency: All businesses employ several resources in achieving their goals and objectives. These resources must be used in a manner that benefits the organisation and as such is very effective in producing results. When organisations are able to perform their duties effectively with very minimum cost, they are described as being efficient, and this is what all organisations should strive to attain.

7. Principle of line of command: Businesses have many subordinates and managers all working together to achieve the organisational goals. However, it is important that subordinates receive their orders from one superior at a time and also be accountable to that particular superior. In instances where subordinates have to be accountable to a number of superiors or to receive directives from different superiors, it usually leads to tension and delays in the performance of tasks which in turn becomes a cost to the business.

8. Principle of span of control: Managers cannot supervise an unlimited number of employees; this does not allow them to properly monitor and assess the activities of these subordinates. This principle, therefore, comes to specify the numerical limit of subordinates that a manager or supervisor can be in charge of. This promotes easy monitoring, evaluation, and assessment of the tasks performed by subordinates, which also leads to efficiency.

9. Principle of communication: Communication is basically defined as the process whereby information moves from one point or person to another. Communication occurs at different levels of the organisation and involves the continuous and systematic process of informing and understanding ideas, opinions, views, and feelings. Effective communication is important to help pass directives, results, corrections, and feedback from one point of the organisation to the other.

4.7.2 Basic Types of Organisational Structure: Formal and Informal

Organisational structures refer to the hierarchy of management and the process that goes into decision-making and implementation to achieve the desired organisational goals (Lewis, 2019). Company leaders or business owners have a responsibility to decide or to determine whether the structure that underlies the operations of their organisations is formal or informal. These choices are not always mutually exclusive as businesses can have an informal structure and still operate with characteristics of a formal structure and vice versa. It is important, however, to have a good understanding of the differences between the formal and informal organisational structure to be able to make the best decisions for your company.

4.7.2.1 Elements of Formal Organisational Structure

In an organisation with a formal structure, the management levels and other divisions within the organisation are clearly spelt out and explained to all employees so they understand how things work in the organisation (Gentile-Lüdecke, Torres de Oliveira & Paul, 2020). Organisational structure may be documented or recorded in the form of an organisational chart to prevent misunderstandings. An organisational chart is a graphical or visual representation of the relationships between each party in the organisation and how the various management levels work. Companies with formal organisational structures usually have a pyramid structure that defines each position hierarchically. It starts with the president of the company, the chief executive officer, and the senior-level managers at the top of the pyramid; the middle-level managers occupying the middle; and the low-level managers at the base of the pyramid. Staff of the company may not be considered in the decision-making process unless there is a need to respond to employee agitation or taking decisions that concerns employee welfare, rights, and remuneration (García et al., 2019). Staff of the company are only expected to implement the decisions made by passing down to the various levels of the workforce.

4.7.2.2 Advantages and Disadvantages of Formal Organisational Structures

The primary advantage that businesses with formal organisational structures enjoy is that the roles and responsibilities of each member of the organisation, from the managers at the top level to the workers at the base of the pyramid, are clearly defined, stipulated, and communicated. This means that each person in the company knows and understands what role they have to perform and how to go about their duties to achieve the desired goals. The formal chain of command also makes it easier to control the work processes since there is a predetermined method of decision-making and implementation of policies and directives.

The main disadvantage of the formal organisational structure is the time it takes for decisions taken at the top level to move down through the middle management level to the lower level staff. Thus, the bureaucratic nature of the structure slows down the implementation of business decisions and activities. Again, since the rigid structure does not allow for frequent interaction between the top management and lower level staff employees, there is sometimes a relationship gap between these two parties.

4.7.2.3 Elements of Informal Organisational Structure

Businesses with an informal organisational structure do not operate under any written document that spells out the rules and regulations within the organisation, the chain of command, and the responsibilities of each party within the company. Within this organisation, employees work according to a system that has proven effective over some time. Informal structures are usually based on the different personalities of employees and techniques or ways of doing things that have been developed and tested over time (Bonanomi et al., 2020). This makes informal structures unique for many companies as it relies on the cooperation between individuals and teams, the relationships developed between employees, and the focus on achieving the goals of the organisation.

4.7.2.4 Advantages and Disadvantages of Informal Organisational Structures

The main advantage of organisations with informal structures is their high adaptability to change especially within emergencies and in ad hoc decision-making situations. In a world where development and change occur frequently, it becomes imperative for organisations to quickly respond to external factors that impact the operations of organisations. Thus, an informal structure makes it possible to make the necessary changes quickly and efficiently.

The primary disadvantage of the informal organisational structure is the tendency for things to become too informal which can result in disorganisation, misinterpreted communication, and confusion. Another disadvantage of this structure is that employees may take advantage of the lack of a formal or official management structure and the freedom that comes with it to arbitrarily make decisions without properly adhering to logical procedures.

4.7.3 Types of Organisational Structures (Functional, Divisional, and Matrix)

Organisations are deliberately set up in ways that will lead to the accomplishment of different goals as the structure employed within the organisation tends to either promote or hinder the progress towards achieving these goals. Both small and large organisations can make higher sales and profits if they are able to properly match the needs of their companies with the structure they employ in their operations. The following subsections will focus on three types of organisational structures, that is, functional structure, divisional structure, and the matrix structure which is a blend of the two (functional and divisional).

4.7.3.1 Functional Structure

The functional structure groups the various portions of the organisation according to the purpose they serve (Tien, 2019). This type of organisation may have, for example, a production department, a sales department, a marketing department, and a human resource department. The functional structure is best suited for small businesses whose individual departments can rely on the knowledge, talents, and experiences of their workers to support themselves. One major drawback, however, of the functional structure is that the easy flow of communication and coordination among departments can be strained or restricted due to the organisational boundaries arising from departments working separately.

4.7.3.2 Divisional Structure

This structure is used typically in larger businesses that have separate smaller groups within the larger organisation (. For example, an organisation which deals in vehicle spare parts can be organised divisionally with a compressor division, a parts division, or even divisions to handle specific needs geographically. The benefit of the divisional structure is that it allows needs to be met swiftly and specifically since each division is able to operate independently of the other divisions that exist within the organisation. A divisional arrangement also has its downsides including communication being inhibited because workers in different parts of the organisation are not working together (Lin et al., 2020). Another downside of this structure is that it is costly to run because of its scope and size. Small businesses can also use the divisional structure on a smaller scale. This could involve having several offices in different regions or tasking different sales teams to work in specific geographical areas.

4.7.3.3 Matrix Structure

The matrix structure is the third main type of organisational structure which serves as a hybrid of the functional and divisional structures (Kiruba Nagini, Devi & Mohamed, 2020). The matrix structure allows organisations to benefit from both the functional and divisional structures, and it is typically used in large, multinational organisations. One disadvantage of this structure is that it sometimes results in a power struggle since a functional manager and a divisional manager is working with similar levels of authority within the same managerial space.

4.7.4 Bureaucratic Organisations

A bureaucratic organisation is a government agency or for-profit enterprise with a rigidly enforced chain of command and strictly regulated operating procedures. It is an administrative system based on policies, rules, and hierarchies in both the public and private sectors (Ouchi, 2019). This system is defined by four specific features.

1. Bureaucratic organisations have a clear hierarchy that defines who has authority and how much of it they have.
2. Bureaucratic organisations create a rigid division of labour or tasks to be performed.
3. They also have rules or laws referred to as policies and procedures, which are inflexible and are accompanied by consequences if not followed cautiously.
4. They are also characterised by impersonal relationships.

Bureaucratic organisations have been described as tight as this is largely because organisations that practice bureaucracy have policies and procedures for every undertaking. Tight control is exerted over the day-to-day activities and operations of the organisation, and if ever there is a need for change, it is slow to take place. Bureaucratic organisations are strict and formal, with graphical representations for every department in the form of organisational charts (Martela, 2019). Each worker knows his role and understands his responsibilities. There is a protocol employed for decision-making, and the control exerted over the operations of the organisation is absolute. Bureaucracy is a term usually attributed to governmental organisations; however, most people encounter bureaucracy in one form or another or even work in bureaucracies (Kanter, 2019).

One of the merits of a bureaucracy is that it creates structures that help make people feel safe and productive. The rigidity of policies and laws that guide and direct workers in bureaucratic organisations ensures the well-being of the business and the society also. When challenges arise, the structures put in place make it possible to make the necessary corrections before the rest of the business or society can be affected (Kallio, Kallio & Blomberg, 2020). One of the demerits of bureaucracies has to do with the issue of time. The act of working with less flexible rules and regulations can be time-consuming. This additional time spent translates into added costs to all parties involved. This phenomenon, in effect, means that the customer bears the higher cost in commercial structures, and the taxpayer has an extra burden to bear in relation to governance.

4.7.4.1 Structure of Bureaucratic Organisations

Bureaucratic organisations are characterised by many levels of management, which usually starts at the top with the chief executive officer or the president of the company. This person sits at the top of the organisational pyramid with the vice-president below who reports to the chief executive officer (CEO). The directors report to the vice-president with the managers reporting to the directors, and it continues down the organisational structure The structure of such organisations is essentially a pyramid with an increased number of employees at different levels as one goes down the pyramid. The maintenance of this structure plays a very important role in the proper functioning of a bureaucratic organisation (Kanter, 2019).

4.7.4.2 Power Holders in Bureaucratic Organisations

Power in such organisations is wielded by only a few people. These include the chief executive officer (CEO), chief financial officer (CFO), and chief operating officer (COO), who are referred to as "'c-level'" executives and are also followed by high-level managers. These high-ranking officials essentially determine decisions to be taken in relation to meeting the objectives of the company including policy-related decisions, human resource-related decisions, or financial decisions (Cohen & Hertz, 2020). The push for decisions to be taken needs to go through the organisational hierarchy up to the highest ranking officials, as this process results in making the acceptance of change, and the implementation of change is very slow in a bureaucracy. This is because suggestions, directives, and'feedback have to travel through all the levels between the source of the directive or suggestion and the destination.

4.7.4.3 Administration of a Bureaucratic Organisation

Administrative procedures, policies, rules, and regulations exist in all well-organised bureaucracies. All employees, at one point or another, will have to carry out some administrative responsibilities. In bureaucratic organisations, all policies governing the activities of workers are carefully and deliberately crafted and worded (Döring, 2021). They are then circulated to every member of the organisation, and everyone is expected to follow them. The managers have the job of interpreting the policies and the procedures to their staff to help them understand better what is required of them. These policies and procedures are frequently referred to, and they govern a wide range of tasks done by employees.

4.7.4.4 Impersonal Nature of Bureaucratic Organisations

Individuals in a bureaucratic organisation are valued based on how well they carry out tasks assigned to them, and how well they adhere to the policies of the organisation. Creativity, innovativeness, and individual decision-making are most often than not frowned upon and discouraged (Schaefer, 2019). Strict regulations govern every aspect of running a bureaucratic organisation. Everyone is expected to perform specific tasks assigned to them and to do them well; such organisations typically have titles for nearly every position and all activities are guided by company policies. Bureaucratic organisations are modelled after the idea that the company is a machine and needs to function with well-oiled cogs. The structure of the organisation encourages formality and is close to strict military-like discipline (Hsu & Lamb, 2020). They are indeed the strictest kind of organisation that exists.

4.8 Staffing

Staffing is a purely human resource function. It is the responsibility to staff the organisational structure and with the right personnel for the delivery of the goals and set targets of the organisation. In recent years, the importance of staffing has increased due to technological advancements, business expansion, and the complexity of human behaviour (Anwar & Abdullah, 2021). The primary objective of staffing is to place the appropriate person in the appropriate position, i.e., square pegs in square holes and round pegs in round holes, at the right time. The managerial function of staffing entails manning the organisational structure through the proper and effective selection, appraisal, and development of personnel to fill the roles designed for the organisation structure. Staffing entails human resource planning; recruitment, selection, and placement; training and development; remuneration; performance appraisal; and promotions and transfer.

4.8.1 Human Resource Planning (HRP)

Human resource planning (HRP) is the ongoing process of systematic planning for the future in order to maximise the use of an organisation"s most valuable asset – its quality employees. The planning of human resources ensures the optimal match between employees and jobs, while preventing human resource shortages and surpluses. The HRP process consists of four main steps. They include forecasting labour demand and supply, analysing labour demand and supply, achieving a balance between projected labour demand and supply, and supporting organisational objectives. HRP is a crucial investment for all businesses because it enables them to remain productive and profitable. Human resource planning enables businesses to plan ahead in order to maintain a steady supply of qualified workers. Therefore, it is also known as workforce planning. The process aids businesses in evaluating their human resource requirements and preparing for their fulfilment.

There are some challenges with HRP regardless of how robust and perfect a company develops one. Constantly changing forces, such as employees falling ill, being promoted, and going on vacation, are among the obstacles HRP must overcome.

4.8.2 Recruitment, Selection, and Placement

Recruitment, selection, and placement of human resource are major components of an organisation's overall resourcing strategies, which identify and secure the people required for the survival and success of the organisation (Ray, 2022). Organisational results are enhanced by a more efficient recruitment and selection process. Many employers view recruitment as a difficult task. In reality, however, you can maintain a pleasant hiring process for both your candidates and your colleagues by adhering to best practices. Identifying the vacancy is the first step of any recruitment process. This involves determining precisely what role the new hire must play in order to meet the needs of the business (Kozhakhmet et al., 2022). By identifying your ideal candidate early in the hiring process, you can determine which candidates to pursue. This will help you narrow down your top candidates for the role, thereby saving time and effort in later stages. At this point, the actual search begins; you will implement the strategy you formulated at the outset (Karim et al., 2021). This entails employing any applicable technology, launching advertising campaigns, and highlighting specific facets of your employer brand to attract the best talent. This is when you will post your job to your preferred advertising websites and/or release your marketing materials, such as social campaigns/career websites. Your recruitment software may also provide you with access to an agency portal, allowing you to inform your PSL of the position if you so choose (Abbas et al., 2021).

It is essential to have the proper tools to measure the effectiveness of your attraction campaigns. By tracking the source of your hires, you can more effectively manage your hiring budget in the future and maximise the return on investment of your recruitment campaigns.

The screening phase is a crucial step in the recruitment process. This involves evaluating the qualifications of applicants in order to engage and pursue the most qualified candidates for selection. After selecting the most qualified candidates, it is time to engage them in conversation to determine who is the best fit for the position. Contact is essential at this stage; automating your SMS/email outreach can assist you in keeping candidates engaged and informed throughout the process (Pham & Paillé, 2020). Utilising multiple hiring managers and candidate scorecards can increase consistency in the hiring process and help to combat unconscious bias. Be sure to discuss both the perceived strengths and weaknesses of your candidates and compare them to the requirements for the position that were established earlier in the hiring process. To ensure the success of your new hires, a solid onboarding strategy is essential for ensuring their proper placement (Suwarto & Subyantoro, 2019). Onboarding includes acquainting the candidate with their responsibilities, work environment, and colleagues, as well as providing any necessary training. Positive onboarding has a significant impact on employee retention. The more you make new hires feel at home in your organisation, the more likely they are to advance in their careers and remain with you for the long haul (Becker & Bish, 2021).

4.8.3 Training and Development

Training and development are essential for the development of human resources. It plays an increasingly significant role as a result of the development of technology, which has led to an increase in competition, a rise in customer expectations for quality and service, and a subsequent need to reduce costs (Karim et al., 2019). Globally, it has also become more important to prepare workers for new jobs. Before attributing the increased need for employee training to technology, it is essential to recognise that other factors also play a role (Sheeba & Christopher, 2020). Training is also necessary for the employee's personal growth and advancement, which motivates him or her to work for a particular organisation beyond monetary compensation. Training is also required to update employees on market trends, employment policy changes, and other matters. Thus, the need for change, performance, and advancement are the key pointers for the importance of training and development in the staffing function of management (Al Karim, 2019).

4.8.4 Remuneration

Remuneration of employees refers to the reward or compensation given to employees for their work performance. The fundamental incentive for an employee to perform a job efficiently and effectively is remuneration (Spisakova, 2019). Employee motivation is influenced by pay. Employees' salaries are a significant source of income and determine their standard of living. Employees' productivity and performance are influenced by compensation. Therefore, the amount and method of compensation are crucial for both management and workers (Magnan & Martin, 2019). There are two types of employee compensation: time/hourly rate method and piece rate method.

The time rate method is when compensation is directly proportional to the amount of time an employee spends on the job. Employees are paid a predetermined hourly, daily, weekly, or monthly wage regardless of their output (Koziol & Mikos, 2020). It is a very straightforward method of compensation. It results in minimal resource waste and reduced accident risk. The time rate method produces high-quality work, and it is especially advantageous for new employees because they can gain experience without a salary reduction. This method promotes employee cohesion because employees of a particular group/cadre receive equal pay. There are a number of drawbacks to the time rate method, including the fact that it leads to strict supervision, indeterminate employee costs, decreased employee efficiency because no distinction is made between efficient and inefficient employees, and decreased employee morale. When the work is non-repetitive and the emphasis is more on quality output than quantity output, a time rate system is more suitable.

In piece rate method, an employee is compensated based on the number of units or pieces produced (Svačina, 2021). In this system, output quantity is prioritised over output quality. Under this system, calculating employee cost per unit is straightforward because salaries vary with output. This method requires less supervision, resulting in a lower cost per unit of production. This system improves the morale of the employees as the salaries are directly related to their work efforts. This method is more efficient in terms of labour (Nahar & Zayed, 2019). There are a number of drawbacks to this method, including the fact that it is not easily calculable, leads to a decline in work quality, wastage of resources, decreased employee cohesion, higher production costs, and employee insecurity.

4.8.5 Performance Appraisal

Performance appraisal is the evaluation of an employee's job performance and overall contribution to a company on a regular basis. A performance appraisal, also known as an annual review, performance review or evaluation, or employee appraisal, evaluates an employee's abilities, accomplishments, and growth, or lack thereof (Ali et al., 2019). Companies utilise performance evaluations to provide employees with comprehensive feedback on their work and to justify pay raises, bonuses, and termination decisions. Performance appraisal can occur at any time, but it is typically conducted annually, semiannually, or quarterly. Human resources (HR) departments typically design performance reviews as a means for employees to advance their careers (Alsuwaidi et al., 2021). Performance appraisal provides individuals with feedback on their job performance, ensuring that employees are managing and achieving the expected goals and providing guidance if they fall short. As companies have a limited fund pool from which to award incentives such as raises and bonuses, performance evaluations help determine how to allocate those funds. Performance appraisal provides a method for companies to determine which employees have contributed the most to the company's growth, allowing companies to appropriately reward top performers (Hayati & Sari, 2019). Employees and their managers can use performance evaluations to create a plan for employee development through additional training and increased responsibilities, as well as to identify ways for the employee to improve and advance in his or her career. The performance evaluation should not be the only time during the year when managers and employees discuss the employee's contributions. More frequent communication helps keep everyone on the same page, strengthens relationships between employees and managers, and reduces the stress of annual reviews. Self-assessment, in which individuals evaluate their own job performance and behaviour; peer assessment, in which an individual's work group or coworkers evaluate their performance; and 360-degree feedback assessment, which includes input from an individual, supervisor, and peers (Belsito & Reutzel, 2020).

4.8.6 Promotions and Transfer

A promotion is the advancement of an employee to a higher level position with increased duties, responsibilities, and status. It may or may not be related to the salary increase. Promotion is one of the most effective forms of incentive because it confers greater responsibilities, a higher salary, increased morale, and increased job satisfaction on employees (Pieper, Schröer & Eilerts, 2019). Practically, all employees desire career advancement, and promotion represents an employee"s advancement in the organisational hierarchy. Human resources decisions regarding training, salary increase, promotion, transfer, and separation are based on performance evaluation. Promotion, transfer, and separation functions are effective methods for adjusting the size of an organisation's workforce, while ensuring flexibility and mobility necessary to meet its needs. Opportunities for advancement within the organisation are one of the best incentives a company can offer its employees. Practically, in every organisation, only a handful of employees are always satisfied with their jobs (Bhardwaj, Mishra & Jain, 2021). All humans have a fundamental urge to advance and improve their social standing. This desire motivates the majority of individuals to pursue higher status and higher pay, which in turn improves their standard of living, morale, and job satisfaction. Thus, advancement is one of the most effective forms of incentives, as it fosters a sense of loyalty towards the organisation and encourages employees to exert sincere efforts in the hope of further advancement.

A transfer is the horizontal or lateral movement of an employee from one job, section, department, shift, or plant to another job, section, department, shift, or plant at the same or a different location where his salary, status, and responsibilities remain the same (Na-Nan and Sanamthong, 2020). Transfers typically do not involve a promotion, demotion, or change in job status beyond a transfer from one job or location to another. Some of the reasons for transferring employees within an organisation are to meet the demands of the company's business, at the request of an employee, to correct incompatibilities in employee relations, to accommodate an employee's age and health, to provide creative opportunities to deserving employees, and to prepare the employee for future advancement and promotion (Dziuba et al., 2020). Transfer actually involves job rotation, but it can also be used as a disciplinary action or as a reward.

4.9 Directing

Directing is the aspect of managerial function that enables the several elements of the organisation to function effectively for the achievement of organisational objectives. As planning, organising, and staffing are simply preparations for carrying out the work, directing is regarded as the enterprise's "spark plug" that motivates people to take action (Tien, 2019). Direction is the interpersonal aspect of management that involves directly influencing, guiding, supervising, and motivating subordinates to achieve organisational objectives. It refers to the act of providing leadership and direction to a group of people while keeping the geared up and motivated to be able to achieve organisational goals.

4.9.1 *Leadership Styles*

The act of walking in front of a group of people and leading them effectively from one point to another may seem straightforward, but this comes as a great challenge to numerous people. The real challenge lies in getting followers to buy into your vision and to follow you every step of the way to the destination you wish to lead them to. The task of managing a group of different people with varying goals and aspirations, strengths and weaknesses, capabilities and special talents, and also with different backgrounds and philosophies can be an arduous one. The art of translating these differences into one unified voice poised and motivated towards achieving the organisation"s goals is what we refer to as leadership (Fries, Kammerlander & Leitterstorf, 2021). Leadership styles vary from person to person and in some instances vary by situation. The three basic styles of leadership which are widely recognised are autocratic leadership, democratic leadership, and the laissez-faire leadership.

■ Autocratic leadership style: Managers sometimes trust only themselves and, their abilities, to decide on what"s best for the individuals and organisation. When this happens, these managers prefer to make all the decisions without considering the input of subordinates. Such leaders are the ones referred to as autocratic leaders. They assert authority by making all decisions based on their expertise and personal experience, and they expect their employees to carry out assigned tasks without objections (Erdem, 2021).

■ Democratic leadership style: Some managers like to consider the views and input of their employees or subordinates when making decisions. Such managers retain the authority to determine what eventually happens with the organisation, or which decisions are finally taken concerning the individuals and organisation (Hilton, Arkorful & Martins, 2021). Democratic leaders consider the emotions and opinions of others within the organisation and aim at influencing subordinates to perform tasks that lead to the realisation of organisational goals while keeping them informed about the issues that affect their work. Studies have suggested that followers thrive better under democratic leadership and also that they derive greater job satisfactions as compared to followers under an autocratic leader. The downside of this, however, is that decisions and actions taken may not be the best since other external factors influence the outcomes of activities in the organisation.

■ Laissez-faire leadership style: The French phrase "laissez-faire" loosely translates as "to allow people to do as they choose." This translation rightly describes the laissez-faire leadership style, which is a liberal type of leadership in which leaders employ a hands-off approach and accord their members or followers the freedom to express themselves through decision-making (Jony et al., 2019). This leadership style is basically about leaving employees to work as they please, in an environment where managers exert very little influence and delegate most of the responsibility and power to their subordinates. The laissez-faire leader may offer some advice to employees but mostly give them room and freedom to operate, solve problems they encounter, and make difficult decisions on their own (Ahmed Iqbal et al., 2021).

Leadership can also be categorised as formal or informal based on the structures put in place and the points at which authority is centred in the organisation. Leadership may be described as formal where the leader exerts great influence and employs proper channels of delegating authority. Informal leaders do not have as much power. They mostly offer direction and allow employees to carry out duties. Effective leadership stems from an accumulation of different factors. It is, therefore, necessary to take into consideration all these factors before settling on the type of leadership to employ (Gunawan & Cahayani, 2022).

4.9.2 Theories of Leadership

Over the years, leadership theories have sought to identify the characteristics that make an individual a good leader and also attempt to categorise the qualities that individuals can adopt to improve themselves as leaders taking different situations that leaders find themselves in into consideration. There have been numerous debates concerning the qualities and the psychology of good leadership with some proposing that leadership skills are qualities inherent from birth or extrinsic (Toh & Ruot, 2019). This sought to suggest that people are able to rise to leadership roles owing to certain inborn character traits. Some theories suggest that people who have certain traits are natural leaders with others maintaining that experience and situations can also make leaders out of people.

The study of the psychology of leadership has attracted a lot of interest over the last 100 years with a number of scholars exploring the topic and introducing different theories of leadership in an attempt to unravelling the mystery of how and why people become great leaders (Gardner et al., 2020). Earlier theories focused on the qualities that set apart leaders and their followers, but subsequent theories have considered other variables such as situational factors and skill levels (Day et al., 2021). Here, we will discuss a few of the theories that have been suggested over the years.

■ "Great man" theories: This theory suggests that great leaders are born with certain qualities such as confidence, intelligence, charisma, and some other social skills that make them natural-born leaders (Udueze, 2021). This theory played a role in the popular coinage; "born to lead" and continues to assume that the capacity of a person to lead is inherent – suggesting that true and great leaders are not made but rather born. These theories have often painted great leaders as being heroic, mythic, and often with a destiny to rise to the occasion of leadership when needed. In recent times, the term "great man" has come under scrutiny for suggesting that leadership is only a preserve of males. It is important to note, however, that the term used at the time was because leadership was thought of primarily as a male quality. The great man theories suggest that people cannot just learn how to be great leaders; thus, you are either born a leader or not.

■ Trait theories: The trait theories bear some similarities to the great man theories. It assumes that people become great leaders because they inherit certain qualities that make them better suited to fill the role of leadership (Uslu, 2019). Trait theories have identified similarities in personalities or behavioural characteristics that leaders share. Examples of these traits are self-confidence, extroversion, and courage. The question that continues to challenge the trait theories of leadership is how there are people who possess some or all leadership characteristics – as identified by the trait theories and yet are still unable to become leaders. There are some people with the personality traits associated with leadership, yet most of these people never venture out into positions of leadership. Others who also excel at successfully leading groups lack some of the key traits associated with effective leadership.

■ Contingency theories: According to the contingency theories, no leadership style is considered best in all situations. The contingency theory of leadership, which is also likened to the situational theory of leadership, takes into consideration particular variables related to the environment that could determine the style of leadership that best suits a particular situation (Lartey, 2020). Leadership researchers, like White and Hodgson, suggest that true and effective leadership does not only dwell on the qualities of the leader but is also about striking a good balance between behaviours, needs, and context. Good leaders look out for the needs of their followers, make quick assessments of the situation, and then make the necessary adjustments to their behaviours. The contingency theories teach that the success of leadership depends on a number of variables including the leadership style, the qualities of the followers, and the situation at hand.

■ Situational theories: The situational theories suggest that the choice of leadership style that people make to achieve the best results is based upon situational variables. Different styles of leadership may work best with the decision-making process depending on situational factors (Benmira & Agboola, 2021). For example, in an instance where group members are skilled and have a wealth of expertise, it is wise to employ the democratic leadership style whereas the authoritarian style works best in a situation where the leader has the most experience or is the most knowledgeable.

■ Behavioural theories: Behavioural theories stand in direct contrast to the great man theories. Behavioural theories seem to say that true leaders are made, not born. The behavioural theories of leadership are deeply rooted in behaviourism and do not focus on internal elements or mental qualities, but rather consider the actions of leaders (Salihu, 2019). This theory believes that similar to most skills, people can become great leaders by undergoing training and by learning through observation.

4.9.3 The Peter Principle

People get promoted as a result of their hard work and through the exceptional abilities they possess above their counterparts. These special abilities have been seen to not work to the advantage of some leaders after they are appointed to higher positions, and Laurence J Peter in his book "'The Peter

Principle"' explains how this happens (Benson, Li & Shue, 2019). Laurence states in his book, "'In a hierarchy, each employee tends to rise to his level of incompetence: Every post tends to be occupied by an employee incompetent to execute his duties." He further explains that competent workers more often than not become incompetent supervisors and the same with every junior executive who gets promoted to a senior executive position. Laurence says in his book that competent leaders exist to occupy the tops of every hierarchy, the reason being that they have not yet risen to "'their level of incompetence'." Inasmuch as this statement is not universally proven and does not apply to all organisations or persons, it still has some wider implications in this area.

4.9.4 Leadership Training

Leaders have different abilities which enable them to rise through the ranks and occupy leadership positions, but sometimes may not help them maintain these positions. There is a view that every member of a group can become a good leader depending on the circumstances and how they enable them to perform the function of leadership. This goes to suggest that leadership is not just a personal quality that people have, but instead, it is an organisational function to be taken seriously. Adair's book, "Effective Leadership" (1983), as cited in Adair (2022), suggests a model of leadership training which has gained considerable success and is employed in some management courses. The model is based on circles that overlap each other in the form of a Venn diagram. This approach is a functional leadership approach that recognises the functions or the roles leaders play taking into consideration the basic needs which arise in all leadership situations. In this model, individual needs are set apart from group needs and also from the needs of the task to be done. The job of the leader here is to consider all three elements and to manage each situation by giving suitable priority to each of the variables. The training is organised around the following elements: defining objectives (tasks), planning, controlling, evaluating, motivating, organising, briefing, and setting an example. Adair (2022) considers leadership to be more of the adoption and practice of appropriate behaviour rather than the possession of personal traits.

Different situations affect the priority that has to be given to the different areas of needs. Any good leader can take note of the changing priorities and give some needs preference whenever the situation demands it. The concept which Adair proposes is a contingency approach whereby

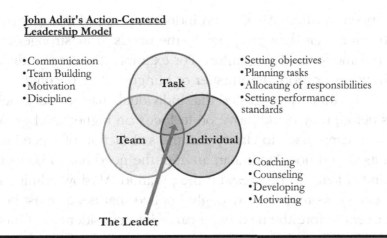

Figure 4.1   John Adair's functional (action-centred) leadership approach (1983, 2022)

the leaders' action is very adaptive and depends largely on the overall situation.

4.9.5 Motivation

4.9.5.1 Maslow's Hierarchy of Needs

Maslow's hierarchy of needs is one of the most common theories of motivation. The theory was introduced by Abraham Maslow and is made up of a five-stage model of the needs of humans (Maslow & Lewis, 1987). These five stages are usually represented in the form of a hierarchy within a pyramid. The needs start with the most basic needs at the bottom and increase with importance as they move up the pyramid. The needs are physiological or physical needs, safety needs, social needs, esteem needs, and finally self-actualisation needs. According to Maslow, humans seek to satisfy the needs at the bottom of the pyramid before they can focus on satisfying the needs higher on the pyramid.

4.9.5.2 Deficiency Needs vs. Growth Needs

Maslow's five-stage model of motivation can further be categorised into deficiency needs and growth needs. The first four stages (physiological, safety, social needs, and esteem needs) are classified under deficiency needs, while the top level (self-actualisation needs) is referred to as growth or being needs. Deficiency needs come up as a result of an individual feeling a sense of deprivation, which usually serves as a push or motivation until these needs have been satisfied. Also, when individuals spend a longer period without satisfying their deficiency needs, the needs grow stronger and usually result in some form of discomfort. For example, the more individuals stay without water or food, the thirstier or hungrier they become.

Maslow (1943) initially suggested that individuals had to meet their lower level needs before they could move on to focus on higher level growth needs. He later came back to clarify that the satisfaction of a need is not absolute in itself and does not mean an end, the need has to be met fully before the individual can progress up the pyramid. Maslow admitted that his earlier statements may have wrongly implied that needs must be satisfied 100 per cent before the next need came into consideration (Maslow and Lewis 1987). When deficiency needs are met satisfactorily, they go away and the individual can direct his energies towards attaining the next set of needs that have to be satisfied. These needs then become our priorities. In contrast, growth needs only grow stronger and are felt even more once the individual engages them. Growth needs come up not as a result of lack or deprivation but rather from ambition and the individual's desire to grow as a person. It is only after the needs have been met satisfactorily that the individual may be able to aspire towards the highest level of self-actualisation.

The desire to move up the hierarchy from physiological needs towards the level of self-actualisation needs is inherent in every person. It is rather unfortunate that this progression is often affected by an individual''s inability to satisfactorily meet lower level needs. Disruptions, such as ill health and loss of jobs, sometimes cause an individual to fluctuate between the needs at different levels of the hierarchy.

4.9.5.3 *Maslow's Five-Stage Model of Motivation*

Maslow (1943, 1987) stated that people have an innate desire to attain certain needs and that some needs come before others. The most basic need that individuals seek to satisfy first is the need for physical survival, and this need is what motivates our behaviour from the onset. After the first need is met, the need at the next level of the hierarchy continues to motivate us, and so forth as shown in Maslow's hierarchy of needs (Figure 4.2).

■ Physiological needs: These needs, also referred to as physical needs, are the biological needs that all humans require for survival. They include air, water, clothing, warmth, sex, and sleep. Our physiological needs must be satisfied to enable the human body to function optimally.

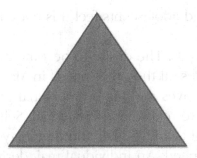

Figure 4.2   Maslow's hierarchy of needs

Maslow considered these as the most important needs since they are the starting point for the satisfaction of all the other needs.

■ Safety needs: According to Maslow, the next needs we focus on are safety needs after satisfying our physical needs. Maslow explains that all individuals have an inherent need for security and protection, and we all want to dwell in a predictable, orderly world which we exert some level of control over. Safety needs include some physiological requirements for survival that make an organism feel safe after they are met. They include the absence of physical threat to the individual (personal security), the absence of infirmity or illness (health and well-being), and access to appropriate medical care in the case of accidents or illness. They also include job security, safe environments, law and order, and stability.

■ Social needs (love and belongingness needs): Social needs follow right after safety needs have been satisfied. This third stage is social and talks about the individual''s desire or need to belong, and this desire to be accepted and to have interpersonal relationships is what motivates the individual''s behaviour at this stage. Some examples include friendship, acceptance, trust, intimacy, and engaging in acts of love. Social needs also refer to the individual''s desire to be a member of a group be it a family, friends, or even at places of work.

■ Esteem needs: These needs can also be referred to as ego needs or status needs. Maslow classified these into two groups: (i) esteem for oneself (dignity, independence, and mastery) and (ii) the desire for reputation or respect from other people. At this stage, the individual is concerned with being recognised, being respected by others, and being regarded in high status. The individual at this point engages in a profession or a hobby that gives them a sense of contribution or value and also allows them to receive recognition from others. According to

Maslow, children and adolescents feel this need for appreciation the most.

■ Self-actualisation needs: The desire to become everything that one is capable of culminates all the other needs in Maslow's five-stage theory of motivation. It involves seeking out personal growth, self-fulfilment, and a strong desire to realise one's potential. Self-actualisation needs vary from individual to individual, and they may focus all their energies specifically on this need. An individual may derive self-actualisation by excelling at a sport, attaining a specific supervisory role, or by bringing about an intervention that tackles a pressing problem in society. It is important to note that self-actualisation is a continual process of becoming a better version of oneself rather than a perfect state one reaches of a "'happy ever after'" (Hoffman, 1988). This goes to affirm what Maslow says that the process of self-actualisation never really ends since people naturally keep aspiring to achieve more.

4.9.6 *Characteristics of Self-Actualised People*

1. They have an acceptance of themselves and others for who or what they are.
2. They look at life through objective lenses.
3. They have higher creativity and an unusual sense of humour.
4. They hold on to strong moral and ethical standards.
5. They can effectively shift their focus to tackling problems, and are not self-centred.

4.10 Controlling

Controlling entails determining whether the activities occurring are in accordance with the actual plans prepared and accepted, the instructions issued, and the guiding principles established. The controlling function also contributes to the effective and efficient application of enterprise resources for the purpose of achieving predetermined objectives (Simons, 2019). Controlling measures the deviation between actual and planned performance, identifies the causes of such deviations, and facilitates the adoption of corrective actions. Controlling, as a managerial process, entails ensuring that all business operations conform to predetermined plans and gives meaning and effect to all other management processes (Prasad, 2020). As a function, controlling is pervasive and continuous.

The function commences as soon as a plan is finalised and formulated and is carried out in a variety of ways from the lowest levels to the highest. Plan-based control is a function that is inherently goal-oriented and requires a clear understanding of one"s own desires.

4.10.1 Controlling as a Process

The controlling process can simply be described as a set of steps a manager uses to determine whether the goals of the organisation have been met. It involves the following steps:

a. Establishing standards to measure performance

This step involves making decisions concerning the goals the organisation intends to achieve within a specific period. These goals may fall within customer satisfaction, production, finance, or employee-related goals (Choong & Islam, 2020).

b. Measuring actual performance

At this step, data collection becomes important in helping to measure employees' actual performance through a set of key performance indicators. which are expected to report on performance in relation to set standards or control measures predetermined by the organisation. Documents such as sales reports, balance sheets, and appraisals reports provide information on employees actual performance.

c. Comparing performance with the standard

This involves making a comparison between actual performance and the set performance standards based on the results from the data collected during the second step of the control process. By employing measuring tools created in the second step, managers compare the current performance to the standards previously set (Tien, 2019). Managers may want to draw comparisons between the companies" sales performance for the previous period to that of the current period. This comparison informs managers on the performance of the sales team, as to whether they are meeting their goals, falling short of them, or exceeding their goals significantly. These are referred to as variances or the difference between what actually occurred and what was expected.

d. Taking corrective action

At this stage, the manager determines what needs to be made, what changes need to be made, and how to go about making a plan to implement the changes. This involves managers looking at a number of factors, making comparisons, and determining which aspects need to be investigated. After the results of the investigation, corrective action may be taken against subordinates for not performing as expected. Managers may decide to assess the work itself to determine whether the work could have been done better with more hands (Yuliaty, 2022). Other questions which may be looked at are the prices of goods and how they affected demand.

4.10.2 *Types of Control Systems*

The primary goal of control systems is to ensure order, and checks and balances within the management systems. The three types of control that can be applied in the management process are as follows:

- Pre-control
- Concurrent control
- Post-control

Pre-control: This is also referred to as preventive or feed-forward control. This type of control is directed at the future as it seeks to help managers prevent or avoid problems rather than find solutions for them after they have occurred (Simons, 2019). It involves predicting challenges that managers could face in the future and determining the corrective steps to be taken to resolve them. It basically seeks to anticipate in advance likely deviations in plans, procedures, or expectations and suggests corrective measures to be taken even before the problem arises. It is a more preferable control tool because it allows for corrections to be made before the output can get affected. The process of pre-control involves the observation and analysis of inputs and processes so as to make adjustments where necessary before the output is obtained. Pre-control devices include organisational plans such as policies, strategies, and procedures.

Concurrent control: This type of control is also known as steering control or real-time control. It is the technique used in controlling activities as they are ongoing or in function. In this system, the manager directs the work of subordinates to ensure that the tasks are performed properly and in tandem with the set standards (Simons, 2019). In the process of functioning, if any deviations occur, they are immediately identified and analysed and the necessary measures are taken to rectify them to prevent any major damages. Concurrent control, as the name suggests, is a continuous process, and adjustments are made as and when they are needed to ensure that all activities are performed to meet or exceed set standards. Some tools employed during concurrent control are inventory control, production control, and quality control charts in organisations.

Post-control: This is also referred to as feedback control or post-action control, and it takes place after the activity is over (Simons, 2019). Management can decide to apply corrective measures after analysing the deviations from planned results that occurred during the execution of tasks. In other words, post-control refers to making adjustments to future actions using information from past performances. Some tools used for this process are standard cost analysis, quality control, employees" performance evaluation, and financial statements analysis. Post-control techniques provide corrective feedback which is very important since it guides and facilitates management to employ the necessary steps to improve the outcomes from future performance.

4.10.3 Some Skills Needed to Be a Successful Manager

Every successful manager will have to master a number of skills. For an entry-level position, the individual needs to have technical competence in the task that they are asked to perform. When advancing, the individual will need to develop strong conceptual and interpersonal skills. The relevance of different skills varies from job to job and company to company, but generally, you will need to have them all to be successful in your managerial career (Rebele and Pierre, 2019). While carrying out your duties as a manager, you will be expected to make efficient use of your time, communicate your ideas, and make sound decisions.

4.10.3.1 Technical Skills

The first basis for which individuals will probably be hired for a job is the technical skills the person possesses; these are the soft or hard skills required which are needed for the early part of an individual"s career (Dzwigol et al., 2020). For instance, if a person majored in marketing and decide to work with an advertising company, the individual will need what was learnt to prepare advertising campaigns. On the other hand, if the degree is in finance, the principles learnt will be used to prepare financial statements and balance the accounts. Technical skills are important at the first-line managerial job and have to supervise and oversee the task performance of your subordinates. Technical skills are primarily acquired through a person"s course of study in a formal education but are developed through job training and job experience.

4.10.3.2 Soft Skills

As the individual climbs up the corporate ladder, you realise that you cannot do everything on your own. You will eventually have to rely on others to help you achieve the goals that you are responsible for. This is why soft skills are very important for managers who rise to mid-level positions (Dolce et al., 2020). These managers operate in a pivotal role since they supervise or oversee the activities of first-line managers while reporting to top-level managers. As such, they need to develop and maintain strong working relationships with people at all levels and in all areas within the organisation. Managers at this level tend to use "people skills" more than most managers, and they use these skills to build trust, foster teamwork, manage conflict, and encourage improvements.

4.10.3.3 Conceptual Skills

Managers at the top are the ones responsible for deciding what is good for the firm as a whole. They do this from a broader perspective and as such rely on their abilities to reason abstractly and analyse complex situations; this skill is referred to as conceptual skills (Miles & Scott, 2019). Executives in senior positions are often called on to think outside the box to develop creative solutions to some complex and even ambiguous issues. Such managers require both strong creative talents and also strong analytical abilities.

4.10.3.4 Communication Skills

Effective communication skills are a necessity for every person. We are judged at all levels of an organisation by our abilities to communicate both orally and verbally (Sotiriadou et al., 2020). Whether you are making a pitch or formal presentation, or talking informally, you will be required to express yourself concisely and clearly. Using poor grammar, talking too loudly, talking too softly, and rambling negatively affect your ability to influence others through speech, and the same goes for poorly written communication. Sending messages that are confusing and riddled with errors do not serve your message well and also do not speak well of you.

4.10.3.5 Time Management Skills

Managers tend to engage in many activities that demand a lot of their time, and this results in their days being filled with interruptions. Managers must develop certain time management skills to avoid the feeling of not accomplishing enough with their days (Alvarez Sainz et al., 2019). A few of the things managers can do to ease the burden on their time include the following:

■ Prioritise tasks, which is giving attention to the things of greater importance
■ Set aside a period for responding to emails and returning phone calls during the day
■ Avoid procrastination
■ Delegate routine tasks to subordinates to perform
■ Insisting on starting and ending meetings on time

4.10.3.6 Decision-Making Skills

Every manager will have to make decisions, whether on their own or in collaboration with a team. A manager must be able to define problems, analyse a number of possible solutions, and select the best outcomes (Abubakar et al., 2019). The decision-making process is very important since it defines the direction in which a manager takes to solve the problems within the organisation and achieve organisational goals.

The skills required by managers vary according to the levels at which they operate. All managers need strong communication, decision-making, and time management skills, thus both technical and soft skills competence in the delivery of their duties. Managers at the lower level need to have strong technical skills which they draw primarily from the courses they have studied and learnt through experience or apprenticeship. Managers at mid-level positions need to have good interpersonal skills to be able to work effectively with others in the organisation. Top managers require strong conceptual skills to determine what needs to be done, when it needs to be done, and how it needs to be done to attain the goals set by the organisation.

4.11 Conclusion

The understanding of management functions is critical to the overall effectiveness and delivery of the goals and targets of any business enterprise. The aforementioned management, that is, planning, organising, staffing, directing, and controlling are interdependent. On the job, however, these functions are largely indistinguishable and nearly unrecognisable. It is necessary, however, to focus on and address each function separately. For the smooth implementation of all, managers are a key force in the successful running of a business due to the multiplicity and complexity of the functions they perform. Team members tend to depend on the decisions managers make or the directives they give to function effectively within the team. This makes the delivery of the management functions a collective effort for the sustenance of the business.

The management function in the post-COVID-19 period remains largely unchanged. Management will have to exercise the functions of planning, organising, staffing, directing, and controlling in order to achieve the set goals of the organisation. More efforts need to be put in, in the performance of these function, as the pandemic has led to a lot of structural changes in organisations.

Management will have to plan and organise activities of the institution they manage so that they can accumulate enough profits to mitigate any unforeseen circumstances or pandemic such as COVID-19 and be able to withstand the shock. Also, management should take the centre stage in directing the staff of the institutions and control the activities of the institution so that the institutions achieve the purpose for which they were established.

References

Abbas, S.I., Shah, M.H. & Othman, Y.H. (2021). Critical review of recruitment and selection methods: Understanding the current practices. *Annals of Contemporary Developments in Management & HR (ACDMHR)*, 3(3), 46–52.

Abubakar, A.M., Elrehail, H., Alatailat, M.A. & Elçi, A. (2019). Knowledge management, decision-making style and organizational performance. *Journal of Innovation and Knowledge*, 4(2), 104–114.

Adair, J. (2022). *Develop your leadership skills: Fast, effective ways to become a leader people want to follow* (Vol. 165). Kogan Page Publishers.

Ahmed Iqbal, Z., Abid, G., Arshad, M., Ashfaq, F., Athar, M.A. & Hassan, Q. (2021). Impact of authoritative and laissez-faire leadership on thriving at work: The moderating role of conscientiousness. *European Journal of Investigation in Health, Psychology and Education*, 11(3), 667–685.

Al Karim, R. (2019). Impact of different training and development programs on employee performance in Bangladesh perspective. *International Journal of Entrepreneurial Research*, 2(1), 8–14.

Ali, Z., Mahmood, B. & Mehreen, A. (2019). Linking succession planning to employee performance: The mediating roles of career development and performance appraisal. *Australian Journal of Career Development*, 28(2), 112–121.

Alsuwaidi, M., Alshurideh, M., Al Kurdi, B. & Salloum, S.A. (2021). Performance appraisal on employees' motivation: A comprehensive analysis. In: Hassanien, A.E., Slowik, A., Snášel, V., El-Deeb, H., Tolba, F.M. (eds) *Proceedings of the international conference on advanced intelligent systems and informatics 2020* (pp. 681–693). Springer International Publishing.

Alvarez Sainz, M., Ferrero, A.M. & Ugidos, A. (2019). Time management: Skills to learn and put into practice. *Education + Training*, 61(5), 635–648.

Anwar, G. & Abdullah, N.N. (2021). The impact of human resource management practice on organizational performance. *International Journal of Engineering, Business and Management*, 5(1), 35–47.

Becker, K. & Bish, A. (2021). A framework for understanding the role of unlearning in onboarding. *Human Resource Management Review*, 31(1), 100730.

Belsito, C.A. & Reutzel, C.R. (2020). SME employee performance appraisal formalization and trust in leadership change. *International Journal of Organizational Analysis*, 28(2), 434–456.

Benmira, S. & Agboola, M. (2021). *Evolution of leadership theory*. BMJ Leader, pp. leader-2020.

Benson, A., Li, D. & Shue, K. (2019). Promotions and the peter principle. *The Quarterly Journal of Economics*, 134(4), 2085–2134.

Benzaghta, M.A., Elwalda, A., Mousa, M.M., Erkan, I. & Rahman, M. (2021). SWOT analysis applications: An integrative literature review. *Journal of Global Business Insights*, 6(1), 55–73.

Bhardwaj, A., Mishra, S. & Jain, T.K. (2021). An analysis to understanding the job satisfaction of employees in banking industry. *Materials Today: Proceedings*, 37(2), 170–174.

Bonanomi, M.M., Hall, D.M., Staub-French, S., Tucker, A. & Talamo, C.M.L. (2020). The impact of digital transformation on formal and informal organisational structures of large architecture and engineering firms. *Engineering, Construction and Architectural Management*, 27(4), 872–892.

Cagle, M.N., Yılmaz, K. & Doğru, H. (2020). Digitalization of business functions under industry 4.0. In: Hacioglu, U. (ed.) *Digital business strategies in block-chain ecosystems: Contributions to Management Science*. Springer, Cham. https://doi.org/10.1007/978-3-030-29739-8_6

Cao, H. & Chen, Z. (2019). The driving effect of internal and external environment on green innovation strategy-the moderating role of top management's environmental awareness. *Nankai Business Review International*, 10(3), 342–361.

Choong, K.K. & Islam, S.M. (2020). A new approach to performance measurement using standards: A case of translating strategy to operations. *Operations Management Research*, 13(3–4), 137–170.

Cohen, N. & Hertz, U. (2020). Street-level bureaucrats' social value orientation on and off duty. *Public Administration Review*, 80(3), 442–453.

Day, D.V., Riggio, R.E., Tan, S.J. & Conger, J.A. (2021). Advancing the science of 21st-century leadership development: Theory, research, and practice. *The Leadership Quarterly*, 32(5), 101557.

Dewanto, D. (2022). TOWS matrix as business strategy of BP. Tapera. *International Journal of Research in Business and Social Science (2147–4478)*, 11(7), 62–77.

Distanont, A. & Khongmalai, O. (2020). The role of innovation in creating a competitive advantage. *Kasetsart Journal of Social Sciences*, 41(1), 15–21.

Dolce, V., Emanuel, F., Cisi, M. & Ghislieri, C. (2020). The soft skills of accounting graduates: Perceptions versus expectations. *Accounting Education*, 29(1), 57–76.

Donkor, A. (2021). Africa's youth unemployment crisis is a global problem. *Foreign Policy*, 1–8. https://foreignpolicy.com/2021/10/19/africa-youth-unemployment-crisis-global-problem/?tpcc=recirc_latest062921

Döring, M. (2021). How-to bureaucracy: A concept of citizens' administrative literacy. *Administration and Society*, 53(8), 1155–1177.

Dziuba, S.T., Ingaldi, M. & Zhuravskaya, M. (2020). Employees' job satisfaction and their work performance as elements influencing work safety. *System Safety: Human-Technical Facility-Environment*, 2(1), 18–25.

Dzwigol, H., Dzwigol-Barosz, M., Miśkiewicz, R. & Kwilinski, A. (2020). Manager competency assessment model in the conditions of industry 4.0. *Entrepreneurship and Sustainability Issues*, 7(4), 2630–2644.

Erdem, A.T. (2021). The mediating role of work alienation in the effect of democratic and autocratic leadership styles on counterproductive behaviors: A study in Ankara OSTİM industrial zone. *OPUS International Journal of Society Researches*, 17(34), 873–902.

Fairlie, R.W. & Fossen, F.M. (2020). Defining opportunity versus necessity entrepreneurship: Two components of business creation. In Polachek, S.W., Tatsiramos, K. (ed.) *Change at home, in the labor market, and on the job* (Vol. 48, pp. 253–289). Emerald Publishing Limited.

Fischer, M., Imgrund, F., Janiesch, C. & Winkelmann, A. (2020). Strategy archetypes for digital transformation: Defining meta objectives using business process management. *Information and Management*, 57(5), 103262.

Fries, A., Kammerlander, N. & Leitterstorf, M. (2021). Leadership styles and leadership behaviors in family firms: A systematic literature review. *Journal of Family Business Strategy*, 12(1), 100374.

Fuertes, G., Alfaro, M., Vargas, M., Gutierrez, S., Ternero, R. & Sabattin, J. (2020). Conceptual framework for the strategic management: A literature review – Descriptive. *Journal of Engineering*, 1–21.

García, G.A., Gonzales-Miranda, D.R., Gallo, O. & Roman-Calderon, J.P. (2019). Employee involvement and job satisfaction: A tale of the millennial generation. *Employee Relations*, 41(3), 374–388.

Gardner, W.L., Lowe, K.B., Meuser, J.D., Noghani, F., Gullifor, D.P. & Cogliser, C.C. (2020). The leadership trilogy: A review of the third decade of the leadership quarterly. *The Leadership Quarterly*, 31(1), 101379.

Gentile-Lüdecke, S., Torres de Oliveira, R. & Paul, J. (2020). Does organizational structure facilitate inbound and outbound open innovation in SMEs? *Small Business Economics*, 55(4), 1091–1112.

Gilboa, S. & Mitchell, V. (2020). The role of culture and purchasing power parity in shaping mall-shoppers' profiles. *Journal of Retailing and Consumer Services*, 52, 101951.

Gunawan, A.S. & Cahayani, A. (2022). Do demographic variables make a difference in entrepreneurial leadership style?: Case study amongst micro and small in creative economy entrepreneurs in Jakarta, Indonesia. *International Journal of Asian Business and Information Management (IJABIM)*, 13(2), 1–6.

Hales, C.P. (2019). What do managers do? A critical review of the evidence. In: Rosemary, S. (ed.) *Managerial work* (pp. 263–290). Routledge.

Hauser, A., Eggers, F. & Güldenberg, S. (2020). Strategic decision-making in SMEs: Effectuation, causation, and the absence of strategy. *Small Business Economics*, 54(3), 775–790.

Hayati, I. & Sari, A.M. (2019). The effect of appraisal performance on employee performance. In *Multi-Disciplinary International Conference University of Asahan*.

Hilton, S.K., Arkorful, H. & Martins, A. (2021). Democratic leadership and organizational performance: The moderating effect of contingent reward. *Management Research Review*, 44(7), 1042–1058.

Hoffman, E.,(1988). *The right to be human: A biography of Abraham Maslow*. Jeremy P. Tarcher, Inc.

Honig, B. & Samuelsson, M. (2021). Business planning by intrapreneurs and entrepreneurs under environmental uncertainty and institutional pressure. *Technovation*, 99, 102124.

Hsu, S.W. & Lamb, P. (2020). Still in search of learning organization? Towards a radical account of the fifth discipline: The art and practice of the learning organization. *The Learning Organization*, 27(1), 31–41

Hu, X., Ocloo, C.E., Akaba, S. & Worwui-Brown, D. (2019). Effects of business-to-business e-commerce adoption on competitive advantage of small and medium-sized manufacturing enterprises. Accra Technical University. https://atuspace.edu.gh:8080/handle/12456789/263.

Islami, E., Sejdiu, L., Hajdini, A. & Imeri, V. (2021). The role of departmentalization, divisional structure and strategic business units (SBUs) in enterprises in Kosovo. *Calitatea*, 22(183), 18–22.

Jauhiainen, T. (2019). Business plan: Establishing a ryokan style inn in Northern Japan. Theseus. https://urn.fi/URN:fi:amk-2019081117780.

Jony, M.T.I., Alam, M.J., Amin, M.R. & Jahangir, M. (2019). The impact of autocratic, democratic and laissez-faire leadership styles on the success of the organization: A study on the different popular restaurants of Mymensingh, Bangladesh. *Canadian Journal of Business and Information Studies*, 1(6), 28–38.

Kahn, M.J. & Baum, N. (2020). Entrepreneurship and formulating business plans. In: Baum, N., Kahn, M. (eds) *The business basics of building and managing a healthcare practice* (pp. 37–41).

Kallio, T.J., Kallio, K.M. & Blomberg, A. (2020). From professional bureaucracy to competitive bureaucracy–redefining universities' organization principles, performance measurement criteria, and reason for being. *Qualitative Research in Accounting and Management*, 17(1), 82–108.

Kanter, R.M. (2019). The future of bureaucracy and hierarchy in organizational theory: A report from the field. In: Pierre, B., James, S. C., Zdzislawa, W. C. (eds) *Social theory for a changing society* (pp. 63–93). Routledge.

Karim, M.M., Bhuiyan, M.Y.A., Nath, S.K.D. & Latif, W.B. (2021). Conceptual framework of recruitment and selection process. *International Journal of Business and Social Research*, 11(2), 18–25.

Karim, M.M., Choudhury, M.M. & Latif, W.B. (2019). The impact of training and development on employees' performance: An analysis of quantitative data. *Noble International Journal of Business and Management Research*, 3(2), 25–33.

Khan, M.A., Saqib, S., Alyas, T., Rehman, A.U., Saeed, Y., Zeb, A., Zareei, M. & Mohamed, E.M. (2020). Effective demand forecasting model using business intelligence empowered with machine learning. *IEEE Access*, 8, 116013–116023.

Kiruba Nagini, R., Devi, S.U. & Mohamed, S. (2020). A proposal on developing a 360 agile organizational structure by superimposing matrix organizational structure with cross-functional teams. *Management and Labour Studies*, 45(3), 270–294.

Kozhakhmet, S., Moldashev, K., Yenikeyeva, A. & Nurgabdeshov, A. (2022). How training and development practices contribute to research productivity: A moderated mediation model. *Studies in Higher Education*, 47(2), 437–449.

Koziol, W. & Mikos, A. (2020). The measurement of human capital as an alternative method of job evaluation for purposes of remuneration. *Central European Journal of Operations Research*, 28(2), 589–599.

Lartey, F.M. (2020). Chaos, complexity, and contingency theories: A comparative analysis and application to the 21st century organization. *Journal of Business Administration Research*, 9(1), 44–51.

Lewis, L. (2019). Organizational change. In *Origins and traditions of organizational communication* (pp. 406–423). Routledge.

Li, L., He, W., Xu, L., Ash, I., Anwar, M. & Yuan, X. (2019). Investigating the impact of cybersecurity policy awareness on employees' cybersecurity behavior. *International Journal of Information Management*, 45, 13–24.

Lin, H., Qu, T., Li, L. & Tian, Y. (2020). The paradox of stability and change: A case study. *Chinese Management Studies*, 14(1), 185–213.

Longva, K.K., Strand, Ø. & Pasquine, M. (2020). Entrepreneurship education as an arena for career reflection: The shift of students' career preferences after a business planning course. *Education + Training*, 62(7/8), 877–896.

Ma, S. & Fildes, R. (2021). Retail sales forecasting with meta-learning. *European Journal of Operational Research*, 288(1), 111–128.

Magnan, M. & Martin, D. (2019). Executive compensation and employee remuneration: The flexible principles of justice in pay. *Journal of Business Ethics*, 160(1), 89–105.

Martela, F. (2019). What makes self-managing organizations novel? Comparing how Weberian bureaucracy, Mintzberg's adhocracy, and self-organizing solve six fundamental problems of organizing. *Journal of Organization Design*, 8(1), 23.

Maslow, A. & Lewis, K.J. (1987). Maslow's hierarchy of needs. *Salenger Incorporated*, 14(17), 987–990.

Maslow, A.H. (1943). A theory of human motivation. *Psychological Review*, 50(4), 370–396.

Miles, J.M. & Scott, E.S. (2019). A new leadership development model for nursing education. *Journal of Professional Nursing*, 35(1), 5–11.

Mondliwa, P. (2020). *Barriers to entry in concentrated industries: A case study of Soweto gold*. HSRC Press.

Nahar, S. & Zayed, N.M. (2019). An analysis of the impact of remuneration on employee motivation: A case study on Unilever, Bangladesh. *International Journal of Family Business & Management*, 3(2), 1–5.

Namugenyi, C., Nimmagadda, S.L. & Reiners, T. (2019). Design of a SWOT analysis model and its evaluation in diverse digital business ecosystem contexts. *Procedia Computer Science*, 159, 1145–1154.

Na-Nan, K. & Sanamthong, E. (2020). Self-efficacy and employee job performance: Mediating effects of perceived workplace support, motivation to transfer and transfer of training. *International Journal of Quality and Reliability Management*, 37(1), 1–17.

Nekhaychuk, D., Kotelevskaya, Y., Nekhaychuk, Y. and Trofimova, V. (2019). The place and role of strategic planning in the business management system. In *Volgograd State University International Scientific Conference "Competitive, Sustainable and Safe Development of the Regional Economy"* (CSSDRE 2019) (pp. 22–27).

O'Connell, M. & Ward, A.M. (2020). Shareholder theory/shareholder value. In: Idowu, S., Schmidpeter, R., Capaldi, N., Zu, L., Del Baldo, M., Abreu, R. (eds) *Encyclopedia of Sustainable Management* (pp. 1–7). Springer, Cham.

Ouchi, W.G. (2019). Markets, bureaucracies, and clans. In: Berry, A. J. Broadbent, J., Otley, D. T. (eds) *Management control theory* (pp. 343–356). Routledge.

Panno, A. (2020). Performance measurement and management in small companies of the service sector; evidence from a sample of Italian hotels. *Measuring Business Excellence*, 24(2), 133–160.

Păunescu, C. & Argatu, R. (2020). Critical functions in ensuring effective business continuity management: Evidence from Romanian companies. *Journal of Business Economics and Management*, 21(2), 497–520.

Phair, J.T. & King, R. (1998). Organizational charts and job descriptions for the advancement office. The Sample File Series. Council for Advancement and Support of Education, 1307 New York Ave., NW, Suite 1000, Washington, DC 20005-4701.

Pham, D.D.T. & Paillé, P. (2020). Green recruitment and selection: An insight into green patterns. *International Journal of Manpower*, 41(3), 258–272.

Pieper, C., Schröer, S. & Eilerts, A.L. (2019). Evidence of workplace interventions – A systematic review of systematic reviews. *International Journal of Environmental Research and Public Health*, 16(19), 3553.

Ponte, S. (2019). *Business, power and sustainability in a world of global value chains*. Bloomsbury Publishing.

Prasad, L.M. (2020). *Principles and practice of management*. Sultan Chand & Sons.

Ramakrishna, N. (2019). Henry fayol's principles of management and it's applicability in contract staffing. *International Journal of Management, IT and Engineering*, 9(3), 168–182.

Ray, R.P. (2022). Human resource management practices in small and medium enterprises. *Patan Prospective Journal*, 2(1), 128–134.

Rebele, J.E. & Pierre, E.K.S. (2019). A commentary on learning objectives for accounting education programs: The importance of soft skills and technical knowledge. *Journal of Accounting Education*, 48, 71–79.

Rehman, S.U., Mohamed, R. & Ayoup, H. (2019). The mediating role of organizational capabilities between organizational performance and its determinants. *Journal of Global Entrepreneurship Research*, 9, 1–23.

Rios, J.A., Ling, G., Pugh, R., Becker, D. & Bacall, A. (2020). Identifying critical 21st-century skills for workplace success: A content analysis of job advertisements. *Educational Researcher*, 49(2), 80–89.

Salihu, M.J. (2019). A conceptual analysis of the leadership theories and proposed leadership framework in higher education. *Asian Journal of Education and Social Studies*, 5(4), 1–6.

Schaefer, S.M. (2019). Wilful managerial ignorance, symbolic work and decoupling: A socio-phenomenological study of 'managing creativity'. *Organization Studies*, 40(9), 1387–1407.

Schouten, G. (2019). *Liberalism, neutrality, and the gendered division of labor*. Oxford University Press.

Sheeba, M.J. & Christopher, P.B. (2020). Exploring the role of training and development in creating innovative work behaviors and accomplishing non-routine cognitive jobs for organizational effectiveness. *Journal of Critical Reviews*, 7(4), 263–267.

Simons, R. (2019). The role of management control systems in creating competitive advantage: New perspectives. In: Berry, A. J.. Broadbent, J., Otley, D. T. (eds) *Management control theory* (pp. 173–194). Routledge.

Sotiriadou, P., Logan, D., Daly, A. & Guest, R. (2020). The role of authentic assessment to preserve academic integrity and promote skill development and employability. *Studies in Higher Education*, 45(11), 2132–2148.

Spisakova, E.D. (2019). Position of employee benefits in remuneration structure. *Transformations in Business and Economics*, 18(2), 156–173.

Suwarto, F.X. & Subyantoro, A. (2019). The effect of recruitment, selection and placement on employee performance. *International Journal of Computer Networks and Communications Security*, 7(7), 126–134.

Svačina, P. (2021). Rewarding employee inventions in corporations: Designing a framework to evaluate adequacy of remuneration and offering an optimal remuneration system. *European Journal of Innovation Management*, 24(2), 258–289.

Tharanya, V., Vijayakumar, D.G. & Itumalla, D.R. (2022). Effect of employee engagement practices towards organizational commitment and job performance. *Alochana Chakra Journal*, IX(VI), 33–51.

Tiba, S., van Rijnsoever, F.J. & Hekkert, M.P. (2019). Firms with benefits: A systematic review of responsible entrepreneurship and corporate social responsibility literature. *Corporate Social Responsibility and Environmental Management*, 26(2), 265–284.

Tien, N.H. (2019). *International economics, business and management strategy*. Academic Publications.

Toh, T. & Ruot, K. (2019). The role of traits in the leadership process. Available at SSRN 3441179.

Tomashevska, A. & Hryhoruk, I. (2022). Entrepreneurship with social responsibility as an innovative tool for solving social needs. *Journal of Vasyl Stefanyk Precarpathian National University*, 9(3), 18–27.

Tsao, Y.C., Raj, P.V.R.P. & Yu, V. (2019). Product substitution in different weights and brands considering customer segmentation and panic buying behavior. *Industrial Marketing Management*, 77, 209–220.

Tuominen, S., Reijonen, H., Nagy, G., Buratti, A. & Laukkanen, T. (2022). Customer-centric strategy driving innovativeness and business growth in international markets. *International Marketing Review*. https://doi.org/10.1108/IMR-09-2020-0215.

Udueze, A.E. (2021). The significance of leadership theory in modern management of public institutions. *Journal of Humanities*, 1(1), 9–14.

Uslu, O. (2019). *A general overview to leadership theories from a critical perspective*. Sakarya Universitesi. https://doi.org/10.21272/mmi.2019.1-13.

Van den Bosch, J. & Vanormelingen, S. (2023). Productivity growth over the business cycle: Cleansing effects of recessions. *Small Business Economics*, 60, 639–657.

Van Looy, A. (2020). Capabilities for managing business processes: A measurement instrument. *Business Process Management Journal*, 26(1), 287–311.

Verma, A., Lamsal, K. & Verma, P. (2022). An investigation of skill requirements in artificial intelligence and machine learning job advertisements. *Industry and Higher Education*, 36(1), 63–73.

Vermunt, D.A., Negro, S.O., Verweij, P.A., Kuppens, D.V. & Hekkert, M.P. (2019). Exploring barriers to implementing different circular business models. *Journal of Cleaner Production*, 222, 891–902.

Weygandt, J.J., Kimmel, P.D. & Aly, I.M. (2020). *Managerial accounting: Tools for business decision-making.* John Wiley & Sons.

Yuliaty, F. (2022). Human resources management in developing learning strategies in the new normal era. *JPPI (Jurnal Penelitian Pendidikan Indonesia)*, 8(3), 553–559.

Zhang, H., Veltri, A., Calvo-Amodio, J. & Haapala, K.R. (2021). Making the business case for sustainable manufacturing in small and medium-sized manufacturing enterprises: A systems decision making approach. *Journal of Cleaner Production*, 287, 125038.

Leadership and Management Case Study #1

Peter Weaver Case Study

Peter Weaver does not like to follow the crowd. He thinks groupthink is a common problem in many organisations. This former director of marketing for a consumer products company believes differences of opinion should be heard and appreciated. As Weaver states, "I have always believed I should speak for what I believe to be true."

He demonstrated his belief in being direct and candid throughout his career. On one occasion, he was assigned to market Paul's spaghetti-sauce products. During the brand review, the company president said, "Our spaghetti sauce is losing out to price-cutting competitors. We need to cut our prices!" Peter found the courage to say he disagreed with the president. He then explained that the product line needed more variety and a larger advertising budget. Prices should not be cut. The president accepted Weaver's reasoning. Later, his supervisor approached him and said, "I wanted to say that, but I just didn't have the courage to challenge the president."

On another occasion, the president sent Weaver and 16 other executives to a week-long seminar on strategic planning. Weaver soon concluded the consultants were off base and going down the wrong path. Between sessions, most of the other executives indicated they did not think the consultants were on the right path. The consultants heard about the dissent and dramatically asked participants whether they were in or out. Those who said

"Out" had to leave immediately. As the consultants went around the room, every executive who privately grumbled about the session said "In." Weaver was fourth from last. When it was his turn, he said "Out" and left the room.

All leaders spend time in reflection and self-examination to identify what they truly believe and value. Their beliefs are tested and fine-tuned over time. True leaders can tell you, without hesitation, what they believe and why. They do not need a teleprompter to remind them of their core beliefs, and they find the courage to speak up even when they know others will disagree.

1. What leadership traits did Weaver exhibit?
2. If you were in Weaver's shoes, what would you have done?
3. Where does courage come from?
4. List your three most important values.

Source: https://trainingmag.com/leadership-case-studies/

Chapter 5

Human Resource Management

Learning Outcomes

At the end of this chapter, you will be able to:

- explain how the term "human resource management" (HRM) evolved.
- define HRM and decipher strategic HRM (SHRM) from HRM.
- describe the role of HR and explain HR architecture systems.
- identify the elements of people resourcing and describe the role of learning and development.
- explain performance and reward management.
- describe the nature, elements, and importance of HR policies.

Chapter Outline

- Introduction
- HRM Defined
- Strategic HRM (SHRM)
- Goals of HRM
- Objectives of HR
- HR Architecture
- HR System
- HR Activities
- HR Functions
- Nature of HR Policies

DOI: 10.4324/9781003458524-5

- Importance of Human Resource Policies
- Specific Human Resource Policies
- Conclusion
- References
- Case Study and Case Questions

5.1 Introduction

One of the key resources in every organisation is the people who work in the organisation; hence, if people are managed well, it is likely to result in the development and long-term sustenance of the organisation (DeCenzo et al., 2016; Cole, 1997). Human resource management (HRM) therefore plays a significant role in business establishments. The term "HRM" has recently replaced the terms "personnel management" and "labour management," which evolved around the 1900s (Bril et al., 2021; Matthew, 2021). However, some people prefer to use the term "people management" as they claim that the term "human resources" suggests that people could be used just like any of the other factors of production. Again, the term "human resources" has been found to place people in the same grouping and value as financial, material, and technological resources (Hilorme et al., 2019). Despite these criticisms, it is worth noting that other arguments made in favour of this term view human resources as an asset and capital advantage exploited for the profitability and sustenance of any business venture (Fenech et al., 2019).

5.2 HRM Defined

There are several definitions of HRM, which have been explored over the years. Some authors consider HRM as a strategic, integrated, and coherent method for the recruitment, development, and welfare of people working within an organisation (Zeebaree et al., 2019). HRM is also perceived as all the activities related to the management of employment relations in an institution. HRM has also been defined as the design of management systems to stimulate the productive use of human skills to achieve organisational goals. HRM is also considered as a viewpoint on how human capital is managed through the adoption of practices and policies in organisational design and development, employee resourcing, learning and development, performance, and rewards (Stone et al., 2020). It can be deduced from all these definitions and viewpoints that there are some commonalities that exist which include the fact that HRM concerns people management from recruitment, development, and welfare.

5.3 Strategic HRM (SHRM)

Strategic human resource management (SHRM) is the approach by which human resource (HR) strategies are developed and implemented and integrated into business strategies to support their accomplishment. Elsewhere, SHRM is considered as the process of linking up HR with strategic goals and aims to enhance business productivity and nurture organisational culture, which facilitates novelty and versatility (Collins, 2021; Boxall & Purcell, 2003). SHRM defines how the organisation achieves its goals through human capital via HR strategies, integrated HR practices, and policies. SHRM is not only about strategic planning or individual HR strategy formulation but principally on the integration of the activities and plans of HR and engendering organisational capabilities by recruiting skilled, committed, and motivated staff to undertake, improve, and keep up with the current and emergent competitiveness (Hamadamin & Atan, 2019; Karadjova-Stoer & Mujtaba, 2009).

5.4 Goals of HRM

Institutional HRM has varied goals it seeks to accomplish. These include the following:

- Supporting the institution in achieving its goals through the creation and execution of HR strategies, integrated into the business strategy (SHRM).
- Contributing to the growth of vibrant organisational culture.
- Creating a positive employment rapport among management and staff coupled with an environment of shared trust.
- Encouraging the adoption of moral means of managing people in all institutions.

5.5 Objectives of HR

There are different objectives that HR aims to accomplish. Some of these include the following:

- To accomplish the mission, vision, goals, and objectives of the organisation by harnessing valuable resources such as people.
- To ensure full utilisation of staff potential and capacity by employing diverse methods in job design, recruitment, and placement.
- To ensure staffs' commitment to their work, in their teams and their departments as well as the whole organisation. This will ensure that unwanted conflicts within the organisation are minimised.
- To facilitate the integration and interaction of the organisation's systems, procedures, and activities through a robust organisational culture.
- To support managerial flexibility and adaptability to changes needed in promoting excellence in HRM function to ensure reduction in bureaucracy as well as strict regulations and rules regarding work.

5.6 HR Architecture

The HR architecture of an institution refers to the framework for HRM delivery. It is basically the comprehensive representation of all HRM functions and not just the HR framework of the HR domain (Iravani, Alvani & Hamidi, 2021). HR architecture generally describes the range of HR professionals in the HR role to the network of HR-related rules and activities through the abilities, delivery model, inspiration, and related behaviours of firms' employees.

5.6.1 The HR System

The HR system is one of the most important components of the HR architecture. It comprises the interconnected and mutually helpful HR practices and activities that collectively facilitate the achievement of HRM goals (Boon et al., 2019). The HR system is considered the foremost vehicle in the execution of an organisation's strategy and is mostly considered a significant HR asset. In fact, the HR system is regarded as the HR component that integrates HR viewpoints that describe the predominant values and ideologies accepted in people management. HR systems include the following:

■ HR strategy: It defines the roadmap for each key HRM activity (Azizi et al., 2021).
■ HR policy: It provides direction for the role of HR as well as the implementation guidelines for specific HR areas (Visser, Lössbroek & van der Lippe, 2021).
■ HR practices: These are HR activities adopted in handling and developing human resource and employment relations (Saeed et al., 2019).

The illustration in Figure 5.1 is a presentation of the HR systems:

5.6.2 HR Activities

HR activities have two broad categorisations, namely, transformational (strategic) and transactional activities. Transformational (strategic) activities are focused on cultivating the effectiveness of an organisation and the alignment and execution of business and HR strategies, while transactional activities comprise the key service delivery components of HR, that is, learning and development; resourcing, rewards, and employee relations (Hasan, Islam & Chowdhury, 2020; Patel et al., 2019; Hird, Sparrow & Marsh, 2010). Other schools of thought consider HR activities as seven interconnected activities undertaken within an organisation. These are strategic HR management; equal employment opportunity; staffing; talent management and development; total rewards; risk management and worker protection; and employee and labour relations. These activities are depicted in the diagram below:

5.7 HR Functions

Various functions constitute the field of HRM. These include the following: people resourcing; learning and development; performance and reward; employee relations; and employee well-being (Itika, 2011).

5.7.1 People Resourcing

People resourcing, also known as employee resourcing, refers to activities in the employment process that ensures organisations have the requisite

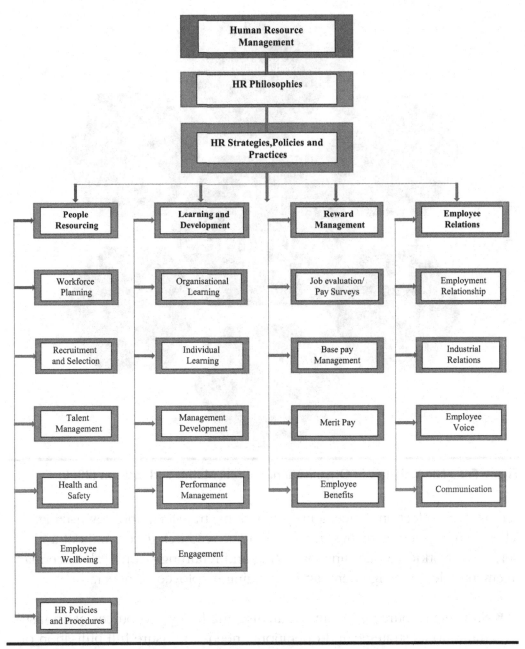

Figure 5.1 Human resource system. Source: Armstrong (2014)

human resource, as it also manages employee issues including absenteeism and turnover (Wilton, 2016; Schneider, 1987; Storey, 1989; Storey, 2007).
Furthermore, people resourcing comprises planning on specific requirements such as the quantity and quality of staff needed for various job groupings and ensuring the effectiveness of the staffing process which involves

Figure 5.2 HR Activities in Organisation. Source: Mathis and Jackson (2008)

recruitment, selection, placement, promotions, transfers, and downsizing. These employment activities involve strategic resourcing; recruitment and selection; workforce planning; attracting and retaining people; absence management; talent management; and managing employee turnover.

■ Strategic resourcing involves matching the human resources of an institution to its strategic and operational needs to ensure full utilisation of the resources. It is also concerned with the careful selection and promotion of the right fit of human resources to the cultural and strategic requirements of every organisation to ensure the attainment of its business goals and competitive advantage (Collins, 2021; Tansley & Tietze, 2013; Torrington et al., 2005). Organisations are able to attract such human resources if they position themselves as the employer of choice and retain them through the provision of improved prospects, rewards, and employment conditions of other employers. Strategic resourcing can also be achieved when the employer pursues a positive psychological contract (that is, the set of mutual but undocumented expectations that pertain to an employee and his employer). Strategic resourcing increases interactions and dedication while creating mutual trust.

▪ Workforce planning is a function of HR that sees to it that an organisation has the right number of human resources who possess the right skills, in the right place and time to get short- and long-term organisational objectives accomplished (Ayandibu and Kaseeram, 2020). Workforce planning is very important for HR planning purposes.

▪ Recruitment refers to the process of searching for and hiring the services of people required by an organisation. Selection, on the other hand, is a step in the staffing process where decisions are made as to which applicants to be selected to fill certain positions (Karim et al., 2021).

▪ Managing employee turnover has to do with adopting policies to ensure that employee turnover, which refers to the frequency with which staff exit the organisation, is minimised significantly (Basnyat and Clarence Lao, 2020). Knowing how often employees leave the organisation and calculating the associated costs are very important because it helps the organisation to estimate future liabilities and plan towards the liabilities. Also, it assists the organisation to understand the reasons behind the exiting of people.

▪ Absence management is concerned with reducing employee absenteeism (typically due to illness, emergencies, or injury) through the implementation of policies and procedures (Alhilali, et al., 2019). To have an impact, these policies and procedures must be communicated to both employees and managers, with management/HR taking an active role in their implementation. Attendance or absence management involves the creation and implementation of procedures and policies adopted to minimise absenteeism.

▪ Talent management refers to the process of certifying that an organisation has the skilled human resource it requires for the achievement of business goals or the protocols and strategies for the methodical attraction, identification, development, retention, and placement of individuals with great potential who offer a certain value to an organisation (Kaliannan et al., 2022). Although the definition discusses "individuals with high potential," which is considered the usual approach, other scholars are of the view that talent management should include everybody for the reason that everybody has a talent that should be managed and not restricted to a few. Talent management activities involve core HR activities such as evaluation of potential, leadership and management development, succession, and career planning.

5.7.2 Learning and Development (L&D)

Learning and development (L&D) refers to the process of ensuring that organisations have knowledgeable, engaged, and skilled workforce they need (Subramanian & Suresh, 2022). It comprises the acquisition of skills and knowledge by individuals and teams through experience; learning through programmes and events which the organisation provides as well as by the tutoring and direction of the line managers. Additionally, individuals learn through self-directed learning activities. The key objective of L&D is essentially to create a conducive environment where people can be stimulated to acquire knowledge and grow.

L&D is made up of four components. These are learning, development, training, and education.

■ Learning is the process by which employees obtain and develop knowledge, skills, attitudes, capabilities, and behaviours. It comprises the change of behaviour through practice and other formal means.
■ Development has to do with the growth of a person's capability and potential via learning and educational experiences.
■ Training is the methodical use of formal means to transfer knowledge and support people to obtain the necessary skills to perform satisfactorily on their jobs.
■ Education is the development of the knowledge, values, and comprehension required in every sphere of life rather than just specific activity areas.

5.7.3 Performance and Reward Management

Performance management refers to an incessant process to identify, measure, and evaluate the output of teams and individuals and align their performance with the strategic goals of the organisation (Camilleri, 2021). It is also about how expectations are communicated by organisations and their impact on behaviour to accomplish significant goals. It again entails how the organisation identifies unproductive employees, so they could be assisted through various programmes or personnel actions and further help people understand the meaning of good performance and provide the necessary information to enhance it. Further, it ensures that performance targets assigned to individuals or teams, departments, and sections are correctly set and approved.

Reward management comprises requisite policies, strategies, and practices to recognise how valuable people and their contributions are in attaining the goals of the organisation, the department, and teams (Perkins & Jones, 2020; Harris, 2005). It also entails the design, execution, and preservation of reward and compensation systems aimed at satisfying both the stakeholders' and the organisation's needs for fair, equitable, and consistent operations. Reward management impacts performance by identifying and rewarding great performance. The rewards in management are predominantly non-financial including recognition, enhanced duties, learning and development avenues, and financial rewards.

5.7.4 *Employee Relationship Management (ERM)*

Organisations engage in employee relationship management (ERM) to foster healthy relationships. ERM efforts boost morale, connect team members, and identify organisational pain points (Maheshwari et al., 2020). The application of best practices in conflict resolution and employee engagement by HR teams and leaders creates a safe and interactive workplace culture. ERM forms part of the employer–employee psychological contract. In this regard, several approaches exist for employers to manage employees individually or collectively, for instance, through trade unions. Some of the issues managed by employers also include employment practices and terms, employment or service conditions, and any related employment issues (Kataria et al., 2020).

5.7.5 *Employee Well-Being*

Employee well-being comprises the creation of a conducive work environment, managing people-related issues, and offering pastoral services for individuals and groups. Well-being exists at work when people like their work and are happy; when they are well treated; how they get along with each other; stress management; health and safety; maintaining a work–life balance; effective handling of bullying and sexual harassment issues; instituting employee assistance programmes for individuals; and social services such as restaurant and sporting amenities for groups (Salas-Vallina, Alegre &

López-Cabrales, 2021). The provision of all these by employers collectively exudes feelings of happiness and satisfaction. Employee well-being is key within every organisation since employees have the right to be treated as full human beings who have hopes, needs, and anxieties.

5.8 Nature of HR Policies

HR policies essentially define values and beliefs that organisations attribute to employees. They are the approaches that organisations adopt in dealing with pertinent areas in HRM, which also provide continuous guidance on the mode of application (Atkinson et al., 2021; Mathis & John, 2008). They include a blueprint on how people should be treated, from which managers derive principles which guide them in handling HR matters. These policies must be shared with both management and staff to minimise or curtail the dangers of arbitrary decisions which are likely to demotivate management and staff and negatively impact the performance of the organisation. Ideally, it is advised that organisations develop HR policies that embrace all HRM functions.

5.9 Importance of Human Resource Policies

HR policies are vital for the reasons outlined below:

- They ensure people management within the organisation aligns with corporate values. They are therefore useful in ensuring consistency between the organisational people management philosophy at the operational level in the form of decisions and activities.
- They ensure the development of consistent HRM to serve as a reference point to avoid erratic decision-making within the organisation and enhance trust and confidence.
- They serve as a guide in promoting standardised and fair treatment of employees by management since a lack of it could bring about disparities in employee treatment and subsequent skirmishes.
- They facilitate decentralisation, regulated delegation, and empowerment as the policies provide direction on how some staffing challenges should be resolved.

5.10 Specific Human Resource Policies

■ Specific HR policies cover all HR functions and activities which include recruitment and selection; HR training and development; equal opportunity; reward; and health and safety.

Recruitment and selection policy: This is a policy on the mode of recruitment and the selection process to minimise the potential dangers of prejudice. This policy facilitates guidance on recruitment and selection policy and also helps the organisation to provide guidance on the time and means by which job advertisements should be placed, conditions and priorities for the selection process, dispute handling procedure, and how it will impact other organisational policies (Mukherjee & Yadav, 2020).

HR training and development policy: This policy should indicate clearly its purpose and the level of commitment to following through with the policy continuously to provide value to employees in terms of maximising their potential in their existing and future jobs (Mihardjo et al., 2020). The policy should exhaust all issues associated with preparation for training and implementation.

Reward policy: The reward policy serves as a blueprint for decision-making and actions on issues such as market rate pay, merit pay, internal and external equality, and incentive. This is important in order to attract adequate and qualified staff; promote retention of productive staff; maximise staff performance; be flexible in rewarding productive employees, and discipline unproductive ones (Pham Tučková & Phan, 2019).

Health and safety policy: This policy constitutes a declaration of management's intentions, mode, and guiding principles for employee protection against dangers or hazards at work. It should also highlight how safety is beneficial to the employee and the public alike; safety as antecedence over convenience; the role all managers, team leads, and staff is expected to play in the creation and execution of health and safety processes; and compliance with the necessary legislations (Fan et al., 2020).

Equal opportunity policy: This denotes that qualified potential employees from a protected group should gain employment without any discrimination associated with race, disability, gender, or even age since it is anticipated that policies on equal opportunities may permeate all elements of the employment process such as recruitment, selection, training, promotions, transfers, salaries, leave, and housing, among others. Equal opportunity impacts employees' potential and subsequent productivity; amenability to the constitution; and further laws as well as having a labour force that is representative of the community (Milikić, 2019).

5.11 Conclusion

The human resource management function has evolved to become one of the strategic assets organisations use to enhance profitability, reputation, and increase market share through the exploitation of this asset and factor of production. Organisations achieve their objectives through people; plans and strategies are implemented through people; the vision and mission of an organisation are achieved through people and structures; and systems are operated by people, while policies are implemented by people. The place of people as an integral part of the business process cannot be over-estimated. Organisations will be largely ineffective without people, and for these reasons, it is imperative that the human resource of every organisation is managed through a mutually beneficial relationship between the organisation and its people, with incentivised components such as adequate training, development, competitive remuneration and compensation packages, and the right resourcing to equip the latter for maximum output. This notwith-standing, it is imperative that the right calibre of people with the requisite skills, right attitude, and experience are carefully selected to work for the organisation.

COVID-19 has brought to the fore issues of human resource management. Workers were restricted in their movement during the peak of COVID-19, and management had to reach out to staff through technology as workers worked remotely. Some organisations thought of reducing human resource by automating their processes, but it is not all operations of a business which can be automated. Managing human resources for effective organisa-tional performance is vital.

Management will have to ensure training of all staff to equip them with the needed skills, especially in IT so that the staff will be abreast in the use of modern communication systems such as Zoom and Google Teams. Staff should also be made aware that the traditional system of doing business before COVID-19 has changed and that staff who have a future in institu-tions are those who are prepared to learn new ways of doing things.

References

Alhilali, A.H., Ali, N.S., Kadhim, M.F., Al-Sadawi, B. & Alsharqi, H. (2019). Multi-objective attendance and management information system using computer application in industry strip. *Indonesian Journal of Electrical Engineering and Computer Science*, 16(1), 371–381.

Armstrong, M. (2014). *Armstrong's Handbook of Human Resource Management* (13th ed.). London: Kogan Page, Ashford Colour Press Ltd.

Atkinson, C., Beck, V., Brewis, J., Davies, A. & Duberley, J. (2021). Menopause and the workplace: New directions in HRM research and HR practice. *Human Resource Management Journal*, 31(1), 49–64.

Ayandibu, A.O. & Kaseeram, I. (2020). The future of workforce planning. In: Sulaiman, O. A. (ed.) *Human Capital Formation for the Fourth Industrial Revolution* (pp. 127–156). IGI Global.

Azizi, M.R., Atlasi, R., Ziapour, A., Abbas, J. & Naemi, R. (2021). Innovative human resource management strategies during the COVID-19 pandemic: A systematic narrative review approach. *Heliyon*, 7(6), e07233.

Basnyat, S. & Clarence Lao, C.S. (2020). Employees' perceptions on the relationship between human resource management practices and employee turnover: A qualitative study. *Employee Relations*, 42(2), 453–470.

Boon, C., Den Hartog, D.N. & Lepak, D.P. (2019). A systematic review of human resource management systems and their measurement. *Journal of Management*, 45(6), 2498–2537.

Boxall, P.F. & Purcell, J. (2003). *Strategy and Human Resource Management*. Basingstoke: Palgrave Macmillan.

Bril, A., Kalinina, O., Valebnikova, O., Valebnikova, N., Camastral, M., Shustov, D. & Ostrovskaya, N. (2021). Improving personnel management by organizational projects: Implications for open innovation. *Journal of Open Innovation: Technology, Market, and Complexity*, 7(2), 105.

Camilleri, M.A. (2021). Using the balanced scorecard as a performance management tool in higher education. *Management in Education*, 35(1), 10–21.

Cole, G.A. (1997). *Personnel Management*. Goshport: Ashford Colours.

Collins, C.J. (2021). Expanding the resource based view model of strategic human resource management. *The International Journal of Human Resource Management*, 32(2), 331–358.

DeCenzo, D.A., Robbins, S.P. & Verhulst, S.L. (2016). *Fundamentals of Human Resource Management*. River Street Hoboken: John Wiley and Sons.

Fan, D., Zhu, C.J., Timming, A.R., Su, Y., Huang, X. & Lu, Y. (2020). Using the past to map out the future of occupational health and safety research: Where do we go from here? *The International Journal of Human Resource Management*, 31(1), 90–127.

Fenech, R., Baguant, P. & Ivanov, D. (2019). The changing role of human resource management in an era of digital transformation. *Journal of Management Information & Decision Sciences*, 22(2), 166–175.

Hamadamin, H.H. & Atan, T. (2019). The impact of strategic human resource management practices on competitive advantage sustainability: The mediation of human capital development and employee commitment. *Sustainability*, 11(20), 5782.

Harris, L. (2005). Reward Strategies and paying for contribution. In J. Leopold, L. Harris & T. Watson (Eds.), *The Strategic Managing of Human Resources* (pp. 227–246). New York: FT Prentice Hall.

Hasan, I., Islam, M.N. & Chowdhury, M.A.F. (2020). Transformational human resource management: Crafting organizational efficiency. In: Patricia, O. P., Xi, Z., Kwok, T. C. (eds) *Handbook of Research on Managerial Practices and Disruptive Innovation in Asia* (pp. 264–281). IGI Global.

Hilorme, T., Perevozova, I., Shpak, L., Mokhnenko, A. & Korovchuk, Y. (2019). Human capital cost accounting in the company management system. *Academy of Accounting and Financial Studies Journal*, 23, 1–6.

Hird, M., Sparrow, P. & Marsh, C. (2010). HR structures: Are they working? In P. Sparrow, A. Hesketh, M. Hird & C. Cooper (Eds.), *Leading HR* (pp. 23–45). Basingstoke: Palgrave Macmillan.

Iravani, M., Alvani, S.M. & Hamidi, N. (2021). Identify the dimensions of the positive-behavior based human resource architecture model. *Public Policy in Administration*, 12(3), 1–12.

Itika, J.S. (2011). *Fundamentals of Human Resource Management – Emerging Experiences from Africa*. Leiden: African Studies Centre.

Kaliannan, M., Darmalinggam, D., Dorasamy, M. & Abraham, M. (2022). Inclusive talent development as a key talent management approach: A systematic literature review. *Human Resource Management Review*, 33(1), 100926.

Karadjova-Stoer, G. & Mujtaba, B. (2009). Strategic human resource management and global expansions: Lessons from the euro disney challenges in France. *International Business and Economics Research Journal*, 8(1), 69–78.

Karim, M.M., Bhuiyan, M.Y.A., Nath, S.K.D. & Latif, W.B. (2021). Conceptual framework of recruitment and selection process. *International Journal of Business and Social Research*, 11(2), 18–25.

Kataria, A., Kumar, S., Sureka, R. & Gupta, B. (2020). Forty years of employee relations–the international journal: A bibliometric overview. *Employee Relations*, 42(6), 1205–1230.

Maheshwari, M., Samal, A. & Bhamoriya, V. (2020). Role of employee relations and HRM in driving commitment to sustainability in MSME firms. *International Journal of Productivity and Performance Management*, 69(8), 1743–1764.

Mathis, R.L. & John, H.J. (2008). *Human Resource Management* (12th ed.). Natorp Boulevard: Thomson South-Western.

Matthew, A.A. (2021). Industrial relations and labour management and productivity: The imperative for sustainable development in Nigeria. *Industrial Relations*, 4(4), 57–67.

Mihardjo, L.W., Jermsittiparsert, K., Ahmed, U., Chankoson, T. & Iqbal Hussain, H. (2020). Impact of key HR practices (human capital, training and rewards) on service recovery performance with mediating role of employee commitment of the Takaful industry of the Southeast Asian region. *Education + Training*, 63(1), 1–21.

Milikić, B.B. (2019). Promoting gender-responsive talent management in police organizations through strategic HRM measuring. *Strategic Management-International Journal of Strategic Management and Decision Support Systems in Strategic Management*, 24(1), 19–29.

Mukherjee, A.S. & Yadav, P. (2020). Impact of recruitment and selection process on employee's job satisfaction in Samsung. *Amity Management Review*, 9(1/2), 27–42.

Patel, C., Budhwar, P., Witzemann, A. & Katou, A. (2019). HR outsourcing: The impact on HR's strategic role and remaining in-house HR function. *Journal of Business Research*, 103, 397–406.

Perkins, S.J. & Jones, S. (2020). *Reward Management: Alternatives, Consequences and Contexts*. New York: Kogan Page Publishers.

Pham, T.N., Tučková, Z. & Phan, Q. (2019). Greening human resource management and employee commitment towards the environment: An interaction model. *Journal of Business Economics and Management*, 20(3), 446–465.

Saeed, B.B., Afsar, B., Hafeez, S., Khan, I., Tahir, M. & Afridi, M.A. (2019). Promoting employee's proenvironmental behavior through green human resource management practices. *Corporate Social Responsibility and Environmental Management*, 26(2), 424–438.

Salas-Vallina, A., Alegre, J. & López-Cabrales, Á. (2021). The challenge of increasing employees' well-being and performance: How human resource management practices and engaging leadership work together toward reaching this goal. *Human Resource Management*, 60(3), 333–347.

Schneider, B. (1987). The people make the place. *Personnel Psychology*, 40(3), 437–453.

Stone, R.J., Cox, A. & Gavin, M. (2020). *Human Resource Management*. Milton: John Wiley & Sons.

Storey, J. (1989). From personnel management to human resource management. In J. Storey (Ed.), *New Perspectives on Human Resource Management* (pp. 1–18). London: Routledge.

Storey, J. (2007). What is human resource management? In Storey, J. (eds) *Human Resource Management: A Critical Text* (3rd ed., pp. 3–19). London: Thompson Learning.

Subramanian, N. & Suresh, M. (2022). Assessment framework for agile HRM practices. *Global Journal of Flexible Systems Management*, 23(1), 135–149.

Tansley, C. & Tietze, S. (2013). Rites of passage through talent management stages: An identity work perspective. *International Journal of Human Resource Management*, 24(9), 1799–1815.

Torrington, D., Hall, L. & Taylor, S. (2005). *Human Resource Management*. New York: Prentice Hall.

Visser, M., Lössbroek, J. & van der Lippe, T. (2021). The use of HR policies and job satisfaction of older workers. *Work, Aging and Retirement*, 7(4), 303–321.

Wilton, N. (2016). *An Introduction to Human Resource Management*. London: Sage Publication.

Zeebaree, S.R., Shukur, H.M. & Hussan, B.K. (2019). Human resource management systems for enterprise organizations: A review. *Periodicals of Engineering and Natural Sciences*, 7(2), 660–669.

Case Study

Satish was a sales manager for Industrial Products Company in City branch. A week ago, he was promoted and shifted to head office as deputy manager – product management for a division of products, which he was not very familiar with. Three days ago, the company VP, Mr. George, convened a meeting of all product managers. Satish's new boss (Product Manager Ketan) was not able to attend due to some other preoccupation. Hence, the Marketing Director Preet asked Satish to attend the meeting as this would give him exposure to his new role. At the beginning of the meeting, Preet introduced Satish very briefly to the VP. The meeting started with an address from the VP and soon it got into a series of questions from him to every product manager. George, of course, was pretty thorough with every single product of the company, and he was known to be pushy and a blunt veteran in the field. Most of the product managers were very clear about George's ways of working and had thoroughly prepared for the meeting and were giving to-the-point answers. George then started with Satish. Satish, being new to the product, was quite confused and fared miserably. Preet immediately understood that George had possibly failed to remember that Satish was new to the job. He thought of interrupting George's questioning and giving a discrete reminder that Satish was new. But by that time, George who was pretty upset with the lack of preparation Satish made a public statement: "Gentlemen, you are witnessing here an example of sloppy work and this can't be excused." Now Preet was in two minds: Should he interrupt George and tell him that Satish is new in that position or should he wait till the end of the meeting and tell George privately? Preet chose the second option. Satish was visibly angry at the treatment meted out by George, but he also chose to keep mum. George quickly closed the meeting saying that he found, in general, a lack of planning in the department and asked Preet to stay back in the room for further discussions. Before Preet could give any explanation to Satish, George asked him "Tell me openly, Preet, was I too rough with that boy?" Preet said, "Yes, you were. In fact, I was about to remind you that Satish is new to the job.". George explained the fact that Satish was new to the job didn't quite register with him during the meeting. George admitted that he made a mistake and asked his secretary to get Satish to report to the room immediately. A perplexed and uneasy Satish reported to George's room after few minutes. George looking Satish straight into his eyes said "I have done something which I should have never even thought of and I want to apologise to you. It is my mistake that I did not recollect that you were new to the job when I was questioning you." Satish was left speechless. George continued "I would like to state a few things clearly to you. Your job is to make sure that people like me and your bosses do not make stupid decisions. We have good confidence in your abilities and that is why we have brought you to the head office. For everybody, time is required for learning. I will expect you to know all the nuances of your product in three months. Until then, you have my complete confidence." George closed the conversation with a big reassuring handshake with Satish.

Questions:

1. Was it at all necessary for George to apologise to such a junior employee like Satish?

2. If you were in Satish's place, how would you respond to George's apology?

3. Was George correct in saying that Satish is there to correct the "stupid mistake" of his boss and George?

4. Would you employ George in your company?

5. Did Preet make a mistake by not intervening during the meeting and correcting George's misconception about Satish?

6. As an HR man, how would you define the character of George – bullying but later regretting? Does his attitude need to be corrected?

7. Would you be happy to have George/Preet as your boss?

Chapter 6

Production and Operations Management

Learning Outcomes

By the end of this chapter, you will be able to:

- define production/operations management and its objectives, types, and factors.
- describe what an operating system is and its concepts.
- state and explain the objectives and scope of production and operations management.
- explain automation and its importance.

Chapter Outline

- Introduction
- Production
- Production Management
- Operating System
- Operations Management
- Scope of Production and Operations Management
- Business Automation
- Conclusion
- References
- Case Study and Case Questions

                                    DOI: 10.4324/9781003458524-6

6.1 Introduction

Traditionally, the function of an organisation could be classified into three basic groups, i.e., production/operations, finance, and marketing. Though the production/operations function forms a core part of the business, this does not necessarily mean that it is the most important function of an organisation. The production/operations function is typically in charge of the management process that seeks to transform a set of inputs (combination of various raw materials) into a predetermined set of outputs (finished goods) as per the goals given to the manufacturing system (Benjaafar & Hu, 2020). Thus, it is the section of an organisation which seeks to add value to products/services. The set of connected tasks in which management engages in the process of manufacturing a product is called production management. On the other hand, the set of tasks in which management engages in the process of services management is termed "operations management." The role of the production/operations function is to generate the supply of output, marketing is to generate the demand for the organisation, while finance is to generate the capital for the organisation. All these groups at one point or another can be evaluated as operating systems.

6.2 Production

Production function is the aspect of a firm which ensures that raw materials are transformed into the needed outputs (products/services) for consumption by society (Garina et al., 2020). Production therefore can be referred to as the process of transforming physical resources into finished goods. Henceforth, production can be seen as a step-by-step value-adding process to an input. Some examples of production are manufacturing of photocopier machines, computers, furniture, and cars. Figure 6.1 depicts a diagrammatic representation of a production process/system.

It is also significant to have a feedback loop linking the information from output to input stages to make sure that the preferred type of output has been produced. Production is a significant function for all industrial or manufacturing organisations, simply because majority of other activities of these organisations alternate around this function.

6.2.1 Production System

This is the aspect of an organisation which is concerned with the mechanism of production in the organisation. It entails the flow of resources

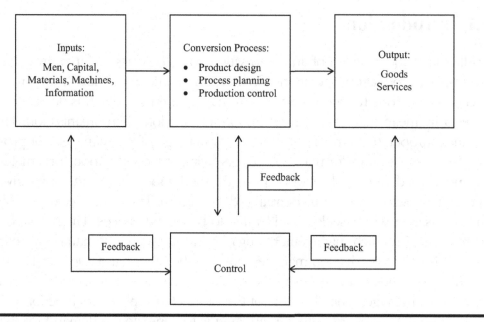

Figure 6.1   Diagrammatic representation of a production system

within a defined system as instructed by the management of an organisation to transform them by adding value (Lanza et al., 2019). The following are some characteristics of a production system:

- Production is a planned activity; hence, each production system has a goal to achieve.
- The system converts different forms of inputs into finished goods for consumption.
- The production system operates together with other organisations' systems.
- It encourages feedback which is needed to boost system performance.

6.2.2 Classification of Production System

The production system of an organisation can be categorised into four, namely, job shop, batch, mass, and continuous production.

6.2.2.1 Job Shop Production

This production system is categorised by manufacturing one or a few volumes of products designed and produced in accordance with the requirement of customers within a given time frame and cost (Mohan, Lanka &

Rao, 2019). This production system is best used when there are a high range of products with small sizes, a need to use all-purpose machines and equipment and a huge stock of materials and equipment. Some of the merits include the use of all-purpose machines which enable the production of different kinds of goods, exploitation of the full ability of workers and the promotion of creativity and innovation. Demerits of this include the frequent set-up changes resulting in higher costs, higher inventory cost, and complication in production planning.

6.2.2.2 Batch Production

This is a type of production that normally happens in instances where large quantities of products are manufactured at the same time (Wang, Lu & Han, 2019). This production system is best applied in situations when plant and machinery are flexible and lower costs are associated with job order production. Merits of this production type include lower cost per unit as related to job order production, sufficient utilisation of plants and machinery, and low cost incurred in purchasing plants and machinery. Demerits may include a complexity in handling materials due to unreliable and longer flows, complication in both production planning and control, and the regular set-up changes which result in higher costs.

6.2.2.3 Mass Production

Mass production happens when there is continuous production of products similar in nature. This production system is usually characterised by large size of production (Kuznetsova et al., 2020). Mass production is best used when there are easy control and production planning, automatic handling of material, and huge volume of products. Some merits of this type include lower cost per unit of manufacturing, requiring less skilled and unskilled labour and low inventory processing. Demerits include halting production when the machinery is faulty, and the demand for huge investment for set-up.

6.2.2.4 Continuous Production

Production equipment is set in accordance with the arrangement of production operations from the first operation to the final output (Kuznetsova et al., 2020). This system of production is best applied in situations where there is complete automation of material handling, manufacturing process following a scheduled order of operations and the planning, and scheduling of repetitive activity. Merits of this type include full automation of material handling, use of low skilled workers in the production line, and lower costs of units due to large production size. Some demerits include limited production differentiation and high investment for setting flow lines.

6.2.3 Types of Production

6.2.3.1 Job or Unit Production

Job or unit production is a type of production that normally arises when a single unit of product is produced to the specification of a customer, e.g., a dress, a car, or a birthday cake. Usually, demand can only be estimated and production schedules prepared when an order is received from a customer. With this type of production, the organisation does not produce and keep goods to be sold later and in the case of raw materials few are kept. Because products are made to the specification of a customer, there is a need for a different variety of machines and equipment in order to do all types of work. As a result, a wide range of skilled labour is needed. An organisation which specialises in this type of production might be able to produce more specific goods. It is usually used by small businesses, individual products or service providers, and premium companies like Dell.

6.2.3.2 Batch Production

This is a type of production that normally happens in instances where large quantities of produce are manufactured at the same time (Wang et al., 2019). This type of production is mostly used by organisations that are into the manufacturing of fast-moving consumer goods (FMCG). Production takes place in batches. With this type of production, the organisations produce and keep it for sale later. Examples of organisations that use this type of production are Nestle Ltd and Unilever Ltd.

6.2.3.3 Flow Production

Flow production happens when there is a continuous production of products that have much or fewer similarities in nature. There is not much time elapsing between the execution of one operation and another, and each machine is continually used for one product and these are often specialised single-purpose machines. There may be a greater expenditure on equipment due to the possibility of a higher rate of machine breakdown. The breakdown of one machine can halt the entire production line, so it is very important to frequently maintain the machine to avoid that.

6.2.4 Factors of Production

In order to produce or manufacture a product, certain resources are needed. These resources are also referred to as factors of production. These resources are combined in different ways by a firm to produce goods for the consumption of people in society. Basically, there are four key factors of production: these are capital resources, natural resources, human resources, and entrepreneurship (Ramey, 1989). Factors of Production

Capital resources refer to resources such as cash, buildings, machines, tools, and technology used to produce goods and services. Natural resources refer to production inputs that are useful just as they appear in nature. Human resources refer to labour, both physical and intellectual contributions of employees. Entrepreneurship refers to the risk-taking process of trying to build a new business.

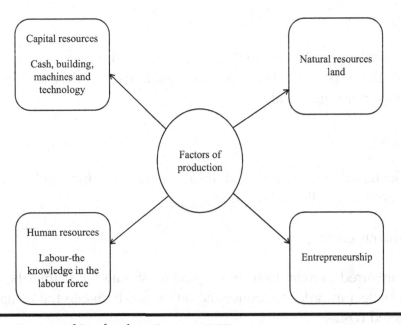

Figure 6.2   Factors of Production (Ramey, 1989)

6.3 Production Management

Production management is the set of connected tasks that management engages in the process of manufacturing a product. Further, it refers to the process of planning and control of the division of an organisation devoted to transforming materials into finished products (Cooper, 2019). Production management blends and converts different physical resources used in the production subsystem of the organisation into finished goods through value addition in a regulated way as per the procedures of the organisation.

6.3.1 Objectives of Production Management

The aim of production management is "to manufacture products that are of the right quality and quantity at the right time and affordable cost."

■ Right quality

Quality can be seen as conformance to standards. The quality of a product is determined from the customer's perspective and not from an organisation's point of view.

■ Right quantity

The organisation should ensure that they produce the right quantity in terms of the number of products they are to manufacture, i.e., they should neither overproduce nor underproduce.

■ Right time

The production department should always make sure that products are manufactured and delivered on time.

■ Right manufacturing cost

The cost incurred in manufacturing a product should fall within the manufacturing budget in order to reduce the difference between the actual and the budgeted cost.

6.4 Operating System

Ray Wild defines operating system as "An operating system is a configuration of resources combined for the provision of goods or services" (as cited by Patil, 2022). An operating system aims to transform inputs into outputs (finished goods). Thus, it transforms physical resources into outputs to satisfy people's wants. The products are of two types, physical goods (e.g., a laptop) and services (e.g., receiving treatment at the hospital).

6.4.1 Concept of Operations

The operation of an organisation can be defined in relation to the kind of technology that it uses as well as its human and managerial procedures. Operations in an organisation can be classified into two, that is, manufacturing and service operations. Manufacturing operations is a transformation procedure that produces a physical output, e.g., a product, while service operations is a transformation procedure that results in an intangible output, e.g. performance.

6.4.2 Distinction between Manufacturing Operations and Service Operations

Below are some features that differentiate manufacturing operations from service operations:

Manufacturing Operations	Service Operations
An output that can be seen, touched, and felt i.e., tangible or physical output.	An output that cannot be seen, touched, and felt i.e., intangible output.
Outputs can be consumed at a later time.	Output is consumed immediately.
There is a little customer contact.	A high degree of customer contact.
Customers are not involved in the transformation/production process.	Customers are involved in the transformation/production process.

6.5 Operations Management

Operations management entails utilising personnel, materials, equipment, and technology as resources. Operations managers acquire, develop, and deliver products to customers based on client requirements and the company's capabilities (Benjaafar & Hu, 2020). Operations management deals with a variety of strategic issues, such as determining the size of manufacturing plants and project management techniques and implementing the structure of information technology networks. Other operational concerns include the management of inventory levels, including work-in-process levels and the acquisition of raw materials, as well as quality control, materials handling, and maintenance policies.

6.5.1 A Framework for Managing Operations

Operation managers are involved in the planning, organisation, and management of activities that affect the overall production process.

■ Planning

Planning refers to activities that establish a course of action and direct future decision-making. In an organisation, the operations manager has to outline the goals, policies, and processes for achieving the objectives of the organisation's operations subsystem. Among the objectives involves role clarification of workers in the production department.

■ Organising

This is concerned with the establishment of how tasks are to be carried out and the flow of communication within the operations subsystem.

■ Controlling

This has to do with checking the plans of the operations system by comparing the actual performance with pre-established performance. This ensures that any deviation in the operations subsystem is detected and corrected as soon as possible in order to avoid any further damage.

■ Behaviour

The operations managers are concerned about how the attitude of their subordinates can influence management's actions. They are mostly concerned about the decision-making ability of their subordinates.

■ Models

As operation managers plan, organise, and control the transformation procedure, they meet many difficulties but they also need to make decisions. Some of their problems can be solved by using a model like break-even analysis to identify break-even volumes.

6.5.2 Objectives of Operations Management

The objectives can be classified into customer service and resource utilisation.

■ Customer service

The focus of the operating system is customer satisfaction. Thus, the operating system is geared towards producing or providing the best service that will meet the needs of the customers.

■ Resource utilisation

The focus of this operating system is the efficient utilisation of resources to satisfy the needs of customers. Ineffective use of resources will lead to the commercial failure of an operating system.

6.6 Scope of Production and Operations Management

The concern of both production and operations management is the transformation of inputs into finished goods by using tangible resources such as raw materials, buildings, facilities, and machinery. Some of the considerations involved in the production and operations management functions are location of facility, plant layouts and material handling, product design, process design, production and planning control, quality control, materials management, and maintenance management.

■ Location of facility

Facility location is concerned with where the operations of the organisation would be situated. Selecting a location is a very important decision as a huge amount of money is needed in constructing the plant and machinery, so an inappropriate place for the plant may lead to a waste of all the money used to purchase the plant and machinery. A location analysis aims to identify the best location resulting in the organisation's utmost benefit.

■ Plant layout and material handling

Plant layout refers to the physical structure of an organisation's facilities. It is the arrangement of divisions within the organisation, workplaces, and machinery in the transformation process. Material handling refers to the "movement of materials from the storage to the machine."

■ Product design

Product design has to do with the transformation of ideas into actuality. As part of an organisation's survival and growth strategy, there is a need to design, develop, and have a continuous introduction of new products into the market.

■ Process design

Process design involves a comprehensive decision-making of an overall process for turning resources into value-added finished products. The important decisions in the design of processes are therefore to evaluate the workflow to transform physical resources into finished products.

■ Production planning and control

Production planning and control is about how the production process will be executed. Thus, it outlines the flow of activities of the production process in advance.

■ Quality control

Quality control can be described as "a system that is used to sustain a preferred level of quality in a product." It is a regular control of different factors affecting the product's quality. Quality control aims to prevent defects at the source. Some objectives of quality control include to increase the companies' profits by making the output more suitable to the customers, reduce business costs by reducing losses caused by defects, produce the best value at a lower price, ensure timely inspection for quality control, and test the manufacturing variability.

■ Material management

Material management is the part of management function which is mainly responsible for procurement and the usage of materials required for the production of products. Some aims of materials management are to reduce the cost of materials, ensure the safety of materials procured, ensure that there is no shortage of materials and tracking new supply sources, and develop friendly relationships with them to ensure continuous supply at reasonable rates.

■ Maintenance management

Plants and equipment are very essential for the manufacturing of products, so they must be maintained on a regular basis to prevent a break down in the production process. Some aims of maintenance management are to attain minimal failure as well as to maintain the plant in an excellent operational state at the minimum likely cost and maintain equipment and other services in a state that allows them to be used at their full capability without stoppage.

6.7 Business Automation

The term "business automation" refers to the use of technology applications to perform repetitive tasks, thereby freeing up employees to perform higher value work. This includes business process automation, robotic process automation, and automation powered by artificial intelligence (Coombs et al., 2020). It is best applied in flow production, e.g., car manufacturing, chemical industry, and other applications with minimum or lesser human interference. It is, of course, restricted by the extent of the market and cannot be generally adopted. By a combination of electronic and magnetic trips, machines' tools are automatically controlled, and thus, work can be automatically transferred to the next stage. Due to automation, there has been an increase in the use of robots in the production process, particularly in the production of motor vehicles. Some benefits of automation include a reduction in machine set-up time and production cost, labour savings as a result of less labour, efficient use of machines, and quality improvement. Some advantages of automation are increased production, enhanced quality, ensures consistency in the production process or product, improved output consistency, reduction in labour costs and expenses, tasks completed are of a high degree of accuracy as compared to manual execution of the tasks, reduces some occupational injuries by encouraging less movement on the production floor, and tasks are performed faster (Ansari et al., 2019). Some disadvantages of automation may include possible security threats, expensive to operate due to high maintenance and development costs, high initial investment cost, and potential to cause redundancy by replacing workers.

6.8 Conclusion

The production or operations function of a business forms a core component of the business. The availability and balance of the factors of production determines to a large extent impact the choice of production system an organisation decides to employ for this business. Thus, the production process must be efficiently managed to ensure the desired finished products. The production or operation function therefore enhances resource utilisation and maximisation to ensure the overall effectiveness and efficiency of the business as a whole.

Even before COVID-19, some businesses had automated their operations and reduced human labour. The COVID-19 intensified the use of machines and robots because these automated processes ensured smooth production devoid of virus infection. People, and for that matter, labour will have to improve upon their skills to make them relevant in the post-COVID-19 period.

Improvement in production and operation management will require businesses identifying the skill gaps in their staff and organising training programmes to bridge the gaps. The staff should also be prepared to undergo training programmes and refrain from considering themselves as having been in the business for a long time, and so they do not need training.

References

Ansari, W.A., Diya, P., Patil, S. & Patil, S. (2019, April). A review on robotic process automation-the future of business organizations. In *2nd International Conference on Advances in Science & Technology (ICAST)*. SSRN. https://dx.doi.org/10.2139/ssrn.3372171.

Benjaafar, S. & Hu, M. (2020). Operations management in the age of the sharing economy: What is old and what is new? *Manufacturing & Service Operations Management*, 22(1), 93–101.

Coombs, C., Hislop, D., Taneva, S.K. & Barnard, S. (2020). The strategic impacts of intelligent automation for knowledge and service work: An interdisciplinary review. *The Journal of Strategic Information Systems*, 29(4), 101600.

Cooper, R.G. (2019). The drivers of success in new-product development. *Industrial Marketing Management*, 76, 36–47.

Garina, E.P., Garin, A.P., Kuznetsov, V.P., Romanovskaya, E.V. & Andryashina, N.S. (2020). Definition of key competences of companies in the "product-production" system. In: Popkova, E. (ed.) *Growth Poles of the Global Economy: Emergence, Changes & Future Perspectives.* (pp. 737–746). Springer, Cham.

Kuznetsova, S.N., Kuznetsov, V.P., Garina, E.P., Romanovskaya, E.V. & Garin, A.P. (2020). Business model of contract productions. In: Kolmykova, T., Kharchenko, E. (eds) *Digital Future Economic Growth, Social Adaptation, and Technological Perspectives* (pp. 21–29).

Lanza, G., Ferdows, K., Kara, S., Mourtzis, D., Schuh, G., Váncza, J., Wang, L. & Wiendahl, H.P. (2019). Global production networks: Design and operation. *CIRP Annals*, 68(2), 823–841.

Mohan, J., Lanka, K. & Rao, A.N. (2019). A review of dynamic job shop scheduling techniques. *Procedia Manufacturing*, 30, 34–39.

Patil, S. (2022). *Production and Operations Management.* Excel Book Private Limited.

Ramey, V.A. (1989). Inventories as factors of production and economic fluctuations. *The American Economic Review*, 79(3), 338–354.

Wang, L., Lu, Z. & Han, X. (2019). Joint optimisation of production, maintenance and quality for batch production system subject to varying operational conditions. *International Journal of Production Research*, 57(24), 7552–7566.

Case Study

Sheena

Sheena had worked for the same Fortune 500 Company for most 15 years. Although the company had gone through some tough times, things were starting to turn around. Customer orders were up, and quality and productivity had improved dramatically from what they had been only a few years earlier due to the companywide quality improvement programme. So, it comes as a real shock to Sheena and about 400 of her co-workers when they were suddenly terminated following the new CEO's decision to downsize the company.

After recovering from the initial shock, Sheena tried to find employment elsewhere. Despite her efforts, after eight months of searching, she was no closer to finding a job than the day she started. Her funds were being depleted and she was getting more discouraged. There was one bright spot, though: She was able to bring in a little money by mowing lawns for her neighbours.

She got involved quite by chance when she heard one neighbour remark that now that his children were on their own, nobody was around to cut the grass. Almost jokingly, Sheena asked him how much he'd be willing to pay. Soon Sheena was mowing the lawns of five neighbours. Other neighbours wanted her to work on their lawns, but she didn't feel that she could spare any more time from her job search.

However, as the rejection letters began to pile up, Sheena knew she had to make an important decision in her life. On a rainy Tuesday morning, she decided to go into business for herself taking care of neighbourhood lawns. She was relieved to give up the stress of job hunting, and she was excited about the prospects of being her own boss. But she was also fearful of being completely on her own. Nevertheless, Sheena was determined to make a go of it. At first, business was a little slow, but once people realised Sheena was available, many asked her to take care of their lawns. Some people were simply glad to turn – the work over to her; others switched from professional lawn care services. By the end of her first year in business, Sheena knew she could earn a living this way. She also performed other services such as fertilising lawns, weeding gardens, and trimming shrubbery. Business became so good that Sheena hired two part-time workers to assist her and, even then, she believed she could expand further if she wanted to.

Questions

1. In what ways are Sheena's customers most likely to judge the quality of her lawn care services?
2. Sheena is the operations manager of her business. Among her responsibilities are forecasting, inventory management, scheduling, quality assurance, and maintenance.
   (*a*) What kinds of things would likely require forecasting?
   (*b*) What inventory items does Sheena probably have? Name one inventory decision she has to make periodically.

(c) What scheduling must she do? What things might occur to disrupt schedules and cause Sheena to reschedule?

(d) How important is quality assurance to Sheena's business? Explain.

(e) What kinds of maintenance must be performed?

3. What are some of the trade-offs that Sheena probably considered relative to:

   (a) Working for a company instead of for herself?

   (b) Expanding the business?

4. The town is considering an ordinance that would prohibit putting grass clippings at the curb for pickup because local landfills cannot handle the volume. What options might Sheena consider if the ordinance is passed? Name two advantages and two drawbacks of each option.

Source: [Production/Operations Management by William J.Stevenson, Irwin/ McGraw-Hill]

Chapter 7

Marketing Management

Learning Outcomes

By the end of this chapter, you will be able to:

- define a market, its characteristics, and elements.
- explain the different concepts in marketing and the marketing process.
- explain Porter's Five Forces model.
- describe the functions of marketing management and environment.
- identify the elements of a marketing plan and research process.
- segment the market for effective targeting.
- manage the product life cycle and clarify the elements of branding.

Chapter Outline

- Introduction
- Market
- Concepts in Marketing
- The Marketing Process
- Porter's Five Forces Model
- Functions of Marketing Management
- The Marketing Environment
- Marketing Planning
- Marketing Research
- Market Segmentation

DOI: 10.4324/9781003458524-7

- The Product Life Cycle
- Branding of the Product
- Brand Equity
- Conclusion
- References
- Case Study and Case Study Questions

7.1 Introduction

The value of an organisation's market underpins its survival. Hence, organisations are under constant pressure to devise strategies that will place them on top of their game and make them competitive (Kim, 2019). Very important processes and activities organisations need to undertake to achieve their marketing objectives include the ability to identify their markets; researching their needs, tastes, and preferences; maximising organisational resources through planning; and finally designing appropriate products to meet those needs (Cortez, Clarke & Freytag, 2021). The marketing process begins with an organisation knowing who its customers are and understanding their role while managing the marketing function to maintain them for the long-term profitability and survival of the organisation.

7.2 Market

For organisations, a market may refer to the demand for a product or service, but generally, a market is a place where sellers present goods, commodities, or services to purchasers or customers and exchange them at a value while taking into consideration other important factors such as demand, supply, and the needs of both parties (Sheth, 2021). A market could also be defined as a place where the potential needs of buyers and sellers are satisfied. A market may be physical or virtual, and it could also be a local market or a global one.

7.2.1 Characteristics of a Market

Markets are primarily for the exchange of trade commodities such as tangible products, intangible services, and money. However, markets have significant features that describe them better. Here are a few of the characteristics of a market:

- A market is a place for the exchange/swapping of goods and/or services for value. The products can be exchanged for money or other commodities depending on the agreement between the two parties.
- A market is a place that fosters innovation and creation.
- It is a place that allows for the negotiation of commodities between purchasers and sellers.
- Markets afford sellers a share of the total demand while giving customers a share of consumption.
- It is a place with a high tendency of covering all the requirements of the customer.

7.2.2 Elements of a Market

The key elements of a market include the following:

- Demand: Markets depend largely on the forces of demand and supply. The buyer first needs a good or a service, and the supplier rightly provides the goods or service to satisfy those needs. The higher the demand for a product, the higher the supply on the market (Ren et al., 2020).
- Seller: The seller offers either a single product or a variety of products or services to buyers, intending to satisfy their needs in exchange for value (Lin & Chang, 2012).
- Buyer: The buyer is the person with needs to be satisfied; someone who requires products or services from a seller and is ready to part with some value as demanded by the seller in exchange for the product (Riyadi & Rangkuti, 2016).
- Place: This is the area where the swapping of goods and services occurs between the buyer and the seller. This could be a distribution outlet or product access point (Bassano et al., 2019). It is always important that the place is convenient for both parties involved in the transaction.
- Product specification: It is always important to state the quantity required and quantity to be supplied, the composition of the good or service, and other important details of the product since individuals

have different tastes and preferences. What is suitable for one person may not necessarily be suitable for another (Cooper, 2019).

■ Price: The price is the amount that is expected in return for the exchange of a good or service (Fauzi & Ali, 2021). For the avoidance of conflict and distortion of the buyer–seller relationship, this price must be fixed at a reasonable rate that satisfies both parties.

■ Government regulation: Every individual is equal before the law, and as such, the government sets some restrictions and regulations that both the buyer and the seller are required to follow (Song et al., 2020). One basic regulation is that the seller is prohibited from putting illegal products up for sale, while the buyer is equally restricted from buying them.

These are the key elements of a market with the power to make or unmake the market. For instance, when the seller or supplier is removed, who then provides the goods or services buyers require to satisfy their needs? In the same manner, if the price for a commodity is absent, at which value do the seller and buyer agree to exchange the product? Each element plays a very unique and important role and as such should always be present to keep the market running effectively.

7.3 Concepts in Marketing

Broadly, concepts in marketing refer to a viewpoint where organisations assess the needs of customers and make decisions in terms of production, sales, and marketing to satisfy these needs better than their competitors (Nunan, Malhotra & Birks, 2020). Before now, marketing concepts were barely utilised by organisations; unlike today, where quite a number of organisations have adopted them. The key concepts are the production concept, the sales concept, and the marketing concept.

7.3.1 Production Concept

This concept enjoins organisations to focus primarily on the products they can produce with utmost efficiency at low cost (Dellaert, 2019). This concept does not take into consideration the needs and demands of customers but focuses principally on production and therefore elicits answers to questions such as: Are we able to produce this product? Are we able to produce enough of this product?

7.3.2 Sales Concept

In the era of the sales concept, businesses looked beyond just focusing on the production of goods and rather made attempts aimed at persuading customers to buy them through personal selling and compelling advertisements (Ancillai et al., 2019). This time round, pre-production information gathered focused more on whether the organisation could sell and account for the goods and not the demand for the product. Not much attention was given to the actual satisfaction of the customer's needs. The concentration of the business was to beat the competition in terms of sales. In the production era, marketing of the goods was done after production; hence, a lot more people perceived marketing as only consisting of "hard selling." To this day, people continue to interchange the terms "marketing" and "sales," erroneously using the word marketing when they are indeed referring to sales (Pal, 2019).

7.3.3 Marketing Concept

The "marketing concept" categorises marketing segments based on size and their specific requirements to satisfy those requirements by manipulating the controllable aspects of the marketing mix (Nikbin et al., 2022). The concept became prevalent in the era of post–World War II, at a time when customers had become selective and therefore made purchases solely based on goods that could keep up with their ever-changing needs. In order to achieve this, organisations attempted to find answers to questions such as what does the customer truly want? Could there be continuous improvement in the face of persistent demand? How do we ensure the satisfaction of our customers? As a result of these probing questions, organisations changed their production model by factoring into it the requirements of customers and again overhauling their business operations which emphasised the unique needs of customers (Lahtinen et al., 2020). Consequently, organisations were able to successfully satisfy the needs of customers over long periods.

Organisations then began to espouse the new marketing concept and that meant setting up distinct marketing departments with the sole aim of satisfying the needs of customers. For most organisations, they operated predominantly in sales departments with extended responsibilities for marketing (Othman et al., 2019). While this phenomenon of sales departments performing marketing functions is prevalent in some organisations today, many others have repositioned themselves to set up marketing departments with global customer attention.

7.4 The Marketing Process

This process comprises the different ways customers benefit from value creation as a means of satisfying their requirements. It consists of a perpetual sequence of activities coupled with interactions between the organisation striving to create value to meet the unique needs of its customers and the customers themselves (Kang, Diao & Zanini, 2021). The marketing process basically consists of the following steps: an examination of the status quo to identify viable opportunities, strategy formulation to serve as a value proposition, taking tactical decisions, executing the marketing plan, and monitoring the results to get the necessary feedback. The process covers the following activities:

7.4.1 Situational Analysis

This is the overall assessment of the current situation the organisation finds itself in, aimed at identifying the prospects to meet the unfulfilled needs of customers. The primary goal of this exercise is to understand the environment in which the organisation operates, to identify the marketing possibilities available, and to gain a better understanding of the organisation's capabilities (Lee & Kotler, 2019).

7.4.2 Marketing Strategy

A marketing strategy is a business's comprehensive plan for reaching potential consumers and converting them into buyers of its products or services. A marketing strategy includes the company's value proposition, key brand messaging, data on the demographics of its target customers, and other high-level components (Katsikeas, Leonidou & Zeriti, 2020). A comprehensive marketing strategy addresses the four Ps: product, price, place, and promotion. After the identification of a viable marketing solution by the organisation, the development of a strategic plan then becomes necessary to serve as a guide in pursuing the choices made (Ngugi, Mcharo & Munge, 2020).

7.4.3 Marketing Mix Decisions

Next, more detailed decisions are crystallised taking into consideration the controllable aspects of the marketing mix. These include decisions related to product development, price, promotional activities, and how the products would be distributed (Mintz et al., 2021).

7.4.4 Implementation and Control

The final step is the execution stage where the marketing plan is implemented, and the outcome or output of all marketing activities is closely observed to allow for the necessary adjustments to the marketing mix to be made per market changes. At this final step, the written strategy is transformed into action and the product is presented using the pre-approved process.

7.5 Porter's Five Forces Model

Michel Porter, well known for his marketing and management thoughts and skills, contributed several valuable theories to modern marketing management. Here, we examine Porter's Five Forces model used for business analysis to establish the reasons for the varying profitability levels across industries; the industry structure of an organisation; and the corporate strategy of the business. Porter recognised the role played by five key forces in shaping markets and industries across the world. The forces are commonly used to measure the concentration of competition, the profitability, and the attractiveness of a market or industry ((Porter, 1997; Abba, 2021).

The model includes the following:

a. The threat of new entrants
b. The bargaining power of suppliers
c. The bargaining power of buyers
d. Industry competitors
e. The threat of substitutes

7.5.1 The Threat of New Entrants

The threat of new entrants discusses the possibility of new competitors entering an already existing market and becoming effective competitors (Porter, 1997). Generally, different products have substitutes with slight variations in quality and price. Low-entry barriers to industry allow new entrants easy access to an organisation's market which poses a threat to the position of the organisation. An industry with strong entry barriers offers a significant advantage to existing markets as it enhances its sales, pricing, and negotiation opportunities. Therefore, existing businesses within an industry are always finding new and sustainable means of warding off potential entrants.

7.5.2 *The Bargaining Power of Suppliers*

Bargaining power refers to the ease with which suppliers can hike the cost of their supplies (Porter, 1997). Bargaining power is usually dependent on the number of suppliers offering those key supplies, the uniqueness, and importance of the supplies as well as the opportunity cost to organisations who decide to switch from one supplier to another. A supplier, also referred to as the producer, is the one who produces the desired product and makes it available to the market. The supplier is not always a single individual, it could be an organisation, a group of people, or any other outlet that makes the product available to the market. The primary function of the supplier is to identify the needs of the client, the market, the society, or the organisation and to produce products that suit the requirements of these interested parties (Porter, 1997). When suppliers of key inputs within an industry are few, organisations tend to be more dependent on them since their options are limited. The scarcity of the inputs gives the supplier the power to arbitrarily drive up the costs of inputs and to advocate for greater gains in his trade. Alternatively, when the suppliers of key inputs within an industry are many or low switching costs exist, an organisation could take advantage of price cuts, hence incur lower costs on inputs and thereby increase their profits (Karagiannopoulos, Georgopoulos & Nikolopoulos, 2005).

7.5.3 *The Bargaining Power of Buyers*

This refers to the power customers wield to drive down the prices of products (Porter, 1997). This power usually rides on the back of the number and relevance of buyers to the organisation as well as the cost to the organisation should it decide to find new customers. The buyer or the consumer is the individual with a need or a demand to be met. This individual exchanges the product made by the supplier as per his requirement, with some valuable commodity that both parties agree upon and is usually referred to as the cost or price of the product. Hence, the buyer needs to be precise in expressing his or her need for it to be adequately met by the supplier (Porter, 1997). An organisation with quite a number of small independent customers will have a better chance of taking more from customers to enhance its profitability. When an organisation has a smaller but influential customer base, it means that the individual customers have more authority to negotiate lower prices and more beneficial deals, which may reduce the profitability of the organisation (Karagiannopoulos et al., 2005).

7.5.4 *Industry Competitors*

The industry competitors are referred to as organisations competing with other organisations within the same market (Porter, 1997). Industry competitors may be a result of supplying the same or similar products that can act as substitutes for one another. For example, we can say that Onga and Maggi are industrial competitors as they are in the same market, that is, food seasoning products. The power that organisations have is usually dependent on the magnitude of their competition in relation to other organisations. The fewer the number of competitors in the same industry, coupled with how many products and services they place on offer, the greater their power (Porter, 1997). On the other hand, the larger the competition, the lesser the power of the organisation. Customers naturally switch to an organisation's competitors when they offer them at lower prices or better deals. However, when competition is low, an organisation can take advantage of its supremacy to sell its products at higher prices and dictate the terms of the deals, so it makes better sales, generates more revenue, and consequentially, makes more profit (Karagiannopoulos et al., 2005).

7.5.5 *The Threat of Substitutes*

Substitute goods and services pose a great threat giving rise to competition in an industry and influencing firms' ability to make maximum profit (Porter, 1997). This is because consumers have the luxury of choice to either purchase one organisation's product or a substitute. When the products of the organisation have close substitutes, customers can decide to forgo the organisation's products, thus weakening the organisation's power. On the other hand, producers or suppliers of goods or services without close substitutes have the power to raise their prices as they tend to dictate terms that are favourable to them, which allows them to make more profits (Karagiannopoulos et al., 2005).

A proper understanding of Michael E. Porter's Five Forces model (Figure 7.1) and its applicability to industries allow organisations to regularly

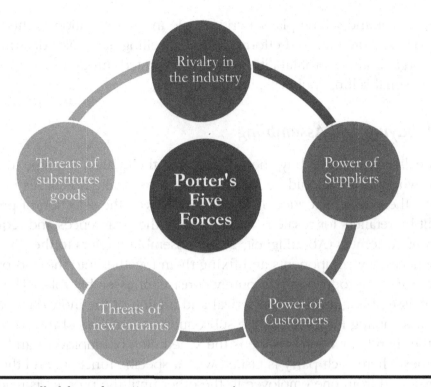

Figure 7.1   Culled from: http://www.masterassignment.com

adjust their business strategies and maximise their resources to make higher returns for their investors. Porter's Five (5) Forces

7.6 Functions of Marketing Management

The term functions of marketing management explain the primary role the marketing aspect of management plays within an organisation (Cartwright, Liu & Raddats, 2021). Marketing management is important and necessary to understand these major roles to facilitate proper comprehension and nurturing of the organisation. Among the major functions are selling, financing, buying and assembling, storage, market information, Standardisation and grading, transportation, and risk-taking.

7.6.1 Selling

Selling, which is at the crux of marketing, comprises convincing potential buyers to buy a product. It involves transferring the ownership of the product from the seller to the buyer (Kumar & Sharma, 2022). Marketing seeks to make a profit and selling plays a critical role in the realisation of this goal. Therefore, the urgency and effort directed at selling is a major determinant of the organisation's profitability. Selling is executed through sales promotion, personal selling, publicity, and advertising.

7.6.2 Buying and Assembling

This deals with what to buy, the quantity and the quality, the time to buy, and at what price it should be bought. Businesses make purchases in a bid to grow their sales or reduce their costs. Moreover, the selection of products bought by retailers for resale is influenced by the preferences and requirements of customers (AbouElgheit, 2022). Assembling refers to the purchase of the necessary components and fixing them together into the end product or a line of production that purely consists of assembly roles. The process of assembling involves the arrival and issuing of the individual parts at the assembling location and the subsequent assembling of the parts. On the other hand, an assembly line is the scheduling of employees and/or machines where each party is tasked with a specific function, and the work is transferred from one employee to the other until the product is ready.

7.6.3 Transportation

Transportation refers to the physical means through which products are transferred from one point to another, usually from the production point to the consumption point (Basalamah et al., 2020). Transportation helps to attain locational value. Transportation is an essential component from raw materials procurement, to the conveyance of the finished goods, through to the access point of the final consumer. Transportation depends on a well-thought-out infrastructure of railroads, waterways, vehicles, airways, and pipelines.

7.6.4 Storage

Storage serves to protect goods from damage, deterioration, loss, and the preservation of surplus goods for future use or consumption. Storage includes keeping products in proper condition from the period they are produced until the time they are required by the production department if they are raw materials or for purchase by customers in the case of finished products.

7.6.5 Standardisation and Grading

Other activities which facilitate marketing include standardisation and grading. First, standardisation is the formulation of standards or specifications for products using their essential physical qualities (Umboh & Aryanto, 2019). Products could be standardised based on quantity as in weight or size, or based on quality as in shape, appearance, taste, material used, and colour. Standardisation centres on promoting uniformity in the production of goods and services. Grading refers to the grouping of the standardised products into distinct classes. It again relates to the further categorisation of products into subgroups consisting of parts with similar characteristics of quality and size such as raw materials, agricultural products and mining products.

7.6.6 Financing

Providing funding to cover the associated costs in getting products from sourcing to production and delivery to the final consumer is mostly known as financing, which forms part of the marketing process (Kumar, 2022). Financing comes in different forms: short, medium, or long term. Accessing financing is necessary to facilitate both working capital and fixed capital and can be sourced from bank loans, owned capital or trade, advanced credit, and personal sources.

7.6.7 Risk-Taking

Risk denotes the likelihood of suffering loss or damage due to some unexpected circumstances. In marketing, risk-taking refers to the act of making financial investments in view of the ownership of goods being held in anticipation of demand (Sheth, 2021). This includes the possible losses that could arise from spoilage usually in the case of perishable goods; obsolescence of the product; and fall in prices, fire, floods, or any other losses that could take place over time. Risk could also be due to deterioration of the product, decay, and accidents, or even as a result of price fluctuation influenced by the variations in demand and supply. The different types of risks marketers could face are classified into physical, place, and time risks, among others.

7.6.8 Market Information

Correct, specific, and timely market information is very essential in supporting marketing decisions besides promoting the overall success of the marketer. The market here refers to the buyers of a product. Market information is derived specifically from market research and broadly from marketing research, which information is used for activities in respect of future marketing planning or product and market development (Varadarajan, 2020). Similarly, this information could be obtained through a single sourcing or from a marketing information system, which primarily collects, analyses, and disseminates current and relevant information to stakeholders on consumers and their changing needs, tastes and preferences, competitors, pricing, market prospects, opportunities, marketing updates, and analysis, among others. This information helps to facilitate effective and informed business decisions. Likewise, marketers require factual and accurate information to plan, minimise challenges, make maximum use of scarce resources, and mitigate losses and risk. Timely and precise market information, for instance, the product's price, quality, availability, and after-sales service opportunities is also helpful to buyers for useful decision-making and cost saving.

7.7 The Marketing Environment

A company's marketing environment consists of the actors and forces outside marketing that affect marketing management's ability to build and maintain successful relationships with target customers (Pimenta da Gama, 2020). In effect, the marketing environment represents a combination of internal and external forces and factors that affect the ability of the business to develop and maintain a good business relationship with its customers. This environment comprises the internal and external environments which affect the operations of the business in one way or the other. Both environments are very critical to the success and survival of the business.

7.7.1 The Internal Environment

The internal environment is organisation specific and comprises anything over which the business has control. This includes the human and other resources of the business, activities, decisions, planning, and any other thing that is undertaken internally within the organisation. This is further categorised into the 5 Ms, namely, men, materials, money, markets, and machinery (Barrachina Fernández, García-Centeno & Calderón Patie, 2021).

The external environment, however, is categorised into micro- and macro-environments.

7.7.2 The Micro-Environment

The micro or task environment deals with factors outside the business, which have direct contact and relationship with the business and affect only the operations and performance of that particular business but for a short period only (Shabbir & Wisdom, 2020). The micro-environment basically refers to the factors involved in manufacturing, distributing, and promoting the product offerings and includes competitors, marketing intermediaries, media, customers, suppliers, stakeholders such as investors, shareholders, partners, publics, and board of directors. The micro-environment directly interacts with the organisation and could possibly affect the activities often undertaken by the organisation.

7.7.3 The Macro-Environment

On the other hand, the macro-environment, also called the broad environment, encompasses larger forces that have the capacity to affect the business as well as the society as a whole, over which forces the business has little or no control (Da Silva & Castañeda-Ayarza, 2021). The six components which make up the broad environment are the demographic, sociocultural, political-legal, technological, physical, and economic environments. It is therefore imperative that a business takes into cognisance these factors and adopts survival strategies to curtail the instability and unpredictability in the business environment.

7.8 Marketing Planning

Marketing planning involves the process of creating a marketing plan which relates to the overall objectives and goals and developing strategies and courses of action to help achieve these objectives (Desai & Vidyapeeth, 2019). The planning process includes setting objectives, goals, or targets; allocating the necessary resources to them; and assigning them to individuals or groups responsible for achieving them. It also includes the assessment of strategic issues including the mission statement of the organisation, the market itself, the business environment, the capabilities of the organisation, and also its competitors.

Marketing planning involves a series of stages which are usually followed sequentially by organisations. Organisations are at liberty to adopt marketing plans that better suit their requirements or specific situations. The most important thing to note is that the process includes objectives development as well as the means and specifications by which the objectives could be achieved effectively and efficiently.

7.8.1 Elements of a Marketing Plan

7.8.1.1 Situational Analysis

■ Mission statement

The mission explains the reason or motive for the existence of the organisation. It is a direct statement that spells out why the organisation has been set up, provides some guidelines for further planning, and provides a general framework for the future activities of the organisation. Experts say that useful mission statements are the ones that encourage employees and customers.

■ Corporate objectives

Corporate objectives refer to the aims organisations set for themselves to be achieved within specific timeframes, usually between one and five years.

■ Marketing audit

Marketing audit facilitates the examination and evaluation of the organisation's marketing strategies, activities, goals, problems, and outcomes. The goal of the audit process is to examine all facets of the business which have a direct correlation to the marketing department (Palav & Jagtap, 2020). It is done at the start of the process and points or intervals during the execution of the marketing process.

■ SWOT analysis

The SWOT of an organisation which represents the strengths, weaknesses, opportunities, and threats is usually established through the marketing audit process. This method of examining the organisation seeks to match the internal strengths and weaknesses (SW) of the organisation against the opportunities and threats (OT) identified after a thorough analysis of the organisation's external environment. In a nutshell, the SWOT analysis assesses the marketing efforts and consequently figures out how it could utilise its strengths to minimise its weaknesses and also maximise its opportunities to reduce its threats (Benzaghta et al., 2021).

▪ Marketing assumptions

Every good marketing plan requires a substantial understanding and knowledge of an organisation's customers. Inasmuch as organisations would want to be able to have all the information about their customers, it is impossible and therefore have to resort to assumptions at times. Organisations assume many different things concerning their customers, and we refer to these as marketing assumptions. A typical example of a marketing assumption is an assumption as to what the needs of target customers would be. Again, one essential ingredient for efficient marketing planning is for top marketing officials to project future outcomes in terms of sales, market trends, and expected cumulative results. Without proper forecasting, there will be no measurable objectives for the sales team to aspire to achieve or look up to, hence, the achievement of the objectives may elude the sales team.

7.8.2 Marketing Objectives

After the situational analysis, it becomes clear the marketing objectives the business needs to pursue. The SWOT analysis and the marketing audit would offer useful leads in this regard. The mission statement would also be a good reminder as to how the objectives should be couched in line with the spirit and letter of the mission statement such that the reason for the existence of the organisation is not missed but rather upheld.

7.8.3 Strategies to Achieve the Objectives

When the objective setting is done, the next step is to determine how they will be achieved, and this process will culminate in a strategy. The Ansoff matrix offers four alternatives for the development of product–market strategies (Igor Ansoff, 1986):

▪ Market penetration: Targeting new segments of the existing customer base with the same product

- Market development: Targeting entirely new markets with the same product
- Product development: Offering new products to the existing customer base
- Diversification: Offering entirely new products to entirely new markets

In order to facilitate maximum results with the achievement of the objectives, there must be an efficient use of limited resources as well as effective targeting and positioning. Hence, the market needs to be segmented before the selected strategies are implemented. Targeting right with appropriate product offers for every segment is the key to increasing sales and reaping maximum financial benefits from the plan.

7.8.4 Tactical Plan and Budget

Once you settle on the appropriate strategy for each of your selected segments, it is now time to develop a tactical plan containing the tactics or short-range actions to facilitate the achievement of the strategies. This is where your extended marketing mix variables come into play: product, price, promotion, place, people, process, and physical evidence also known as 7Ps (Mansaray, 2019). For each of these, a detailed action plan should be developed including the action to be taken, resource provisions, by whom, with timelines, expected outcomes, and contingency plans. All the resource requirements would then be translated into cost centres and subsequently used to develop the budget component of the marketing plan. There are several methods to do this: percentage of revenue method, task method, comparative method, and affordability method.

7.8.5 Implementation and Evaluation – Action Plan

Here, an action plan would have been ready for implementation with tasks and responsibilities already outlined with relevant resources provided working towards a common objective. This phase is also known as the action phase. A marketing plan could be implemented in different ways based on what each activity seeks to achieve. This includes advertising; launching of products, surveys, opening new retail outlets, and collaborations; or just engaging with new and potential customers. This process must however be done with support from every relevant part of the business. It is also imperative to undertake regular assessments by reviewing and updating the entire marketing planning process regularly to introduce flexibility into the plan. As a word of caution, there are likely to be uncontrollable external influences; parts of the plan may not also work well so alternative plans must be developed to curtail any contingencies that may occur in the course of implementing the process.

7.9 Marketing Research

Marketing research is the process by which data are systematically collected, analysed, and interpreted for the use of the organisation in respect of marketing conditions such as the marketing mix elements, market trends, changing needs, tastes and preferences of consumers, and competitive activity, among others (Fisher & Kordupleski, 2019). This process is of great importance since it gives the organisation the chance to identify its target market and get their opinions, suggestions, or feedback about their interests or other factors that may influence their interest in the products or services. It involves the development and interpretation of decision-based information, which will go a long way to influence the actions or inactions of the marketing process. The perception of value changes overtime, hence, what customers perceive or prioritise as a value within a year may differ from their perception in the following year. It is therefore imperative that managers possess the right information required in the different stages of the marketing research process and understand the entire process with its accompanying limitations (Stocchi et al., 2021).

Marketing research can be undertaken by the organisation or a third-party marketing research organisation. Marketing research information can be collected through focus groups, surveys, and product testing. The usual practice is that test subjects receive some compensation for their time, which may be in the form of product samples and/or a small stipend.

7.9.1 The Research Process

It is necessary for every organisation to consistently research the marketing activities of the business, especially where challenges have been cited or pertinent information is needed to pursue a marketing project. The research process includes but is not limited to the steps below.

7.9.1.1 Defining the Problem

The goal for defining the problem is to crystallise the problem on hand by capturing it clearly. This could be done using straightforward questions that would elicit the required information for decision-making. For instance, the research problem on hand may be to establish the extent to which a product taken off the shelves would affect the organisation's market share. This, therefore, calls for research management to solicit information through research for apt decision-making. To achieve this, the researcher may also outline probable research outcomes, which would inform an appropriate action plan. These anticipated outcomes would ensure adequate preparations and consensus on the research objective even before it begins.

7.9.1.2 Designing the Research

After defining the problem the marketing research seeks to unravel, we need to determine the research design that will get us the solution. Marketing research designs can be categorised as follows:

■ Exploratory research

As the name rightly depicts, the purpose of this type of research is to probe or investigate thoroughly the problem on hand. This type of research enables the researcher to clarify the problem further in light of the data collected. This facilitates clarity, with the opportunity to obtain first-hand information and gain further insight into the problem.

■ Descriptive research

This type of research seeks to describe an occurrence and its features. Hence, survey and observation tools are usually used for data collection. In this research, qualitative data could be collected but usually analysed quantitatively using percentages, averages, frequencies, or further statistical investigations to establish relationships.

■ Causal research

Causal research sets out to search for and identify cause-and-effect relationships among variables. This is done through field and laboratory experiments. Any one of the three types of research designs above can be chosen for the research based on the purpose of the research.

7.9.1.3 Data Types and Sources

Data types can be described as the different attributes upon which a given data are classified into different categories. The data types and sources can be categorised into secondary or primary data.

7.9.1.3.1 Secondary Data

Secondary data describe data sourced in the past for a specific use but could be used in a current study. Secondary data could be sourced both internally within an organisation or externally, outside the organisation. Examples of secondary data include information from organisational documentation like reports or external data like published data, national census reports, and reports from government agencies. Data collected from a secondary source are less costly and time-saving. The main disadvantage of this data type is that it may not be very suitable or accurate enough for a different study.

7.9.1.3.2 Primary Data

Secondary data yield optimal results when supported with primary data. Typically, primary data are sourced originally for a specific use or study. Primary data can be collected through observation, survey, interview, or experimentation. This facilitates the acquisition of information from credible sources but the quality or veracity of the information, however, cannot be determined. A common instrument for collecting primary data is a question-naire, which contains predominantly a set of probing questions on the topic under study. The collected data are further analysed and interpreted in light of the research purpose and objectives and a report is produced.

7.10 Market Segmentation

Market segmentation is the regrouping of an organisation's market into sub-segments for efficient and cost-effective targeting with a unique and appro-priate marketing mix (Antika, 2023). For example, Hindustan Unilever (HUL) produces a variety of soaps for different market segments such as "Surf Excel" for the upper class, "Rin" for the middle class, and "Sunlight/Wheel" for the lower class. Marketing segmentation is very useful as:

■ It allows the organisation to plan and maximise resources by providing customised products and services to each segment.
■ It helps with target market selection.
■ It enhances and directs marketing efforts by knowing the market closely with their changing needs, tastes, and preferences.
■ It helps provide each segment the needed attention and helps tap the full potential of the market.
■ It helps maintain competitiveness and enhances customer database management.
■ It facilitates coordination between the organisation and its customers.
■ The strengths and weaknesses of the organisation are also brought to bear to facilitate corrective action.

7.11 The Product Life Cycle

When the market is segmented, the organisation has to do target marketing and select some of the segments based on several factors including the financial value they would offer the organisation, the location, and the resource requirements, among others (Leng et al., 2020). Once this is done, suitable products need to be designed to meet the needs of the segments.

A product's life cycle is in four phases, namely, the introduction, growth, maturity, and decline. The introductory stage is when the product is new to the market and therefore not well known. Demand is low hence the low sales return little profit. Marketing and promotional activities must therefore be enhanced to expand sales and propel the growth of the product. At the growth stage, the product begins to experience some gains through a higher demand and increased market share. Competition also begins to tighten up. Expenses on promotion and marketing activities increase further, and sales pick up gradually as the organisation begins to see profits although pricing is maintained (Wang et al., 2021).

At the maturity phase, the product is at its peak and demand is high with soaring promotional spending and competition is keen at this point. There are price cuts to maintain the market share so profits begin to fall. The fourth and last stage of the cycle is the decline phase. The demand for the product drops, and there are further price cuts by the organisation in an attempt to maintain the customer base (Zhang et al., 2019). There is stiff competition from alternative products and innovative strategies need to be applied by the organisation to hold its head above the waters for survival.

Demand, sales, and profits fall to the barest minimum, and the product takes a nose dive.

7.12 Branding of the Product

Branding is described as a name, concept, symbol, logo, or anything which differentiates the product of an organisation from those of its competitors (Hao et al., 2021). Branding aims to promote a product and is essential in many ways in that it makes the promotion process easy, increases the rate of success in advertising; imprints the product' image in the minds of customers, which they can relate to; represents the organisation; creates product loyalty; stabilises sales; differentiates the product from other products in the market; makes the introduction of a new product easier; and keeps a product stabilised in the market (Kim & Sullivan, 2019)

7.12.1 Branding Strategies

Branding strategy can be divided into producer and middleman strategies (Tran & Rudolf, 2022). The producer strategies considers marketing under the producer's brand and developing a market preference for branded parts or materials, whereas the middleman strategy the manufacturer uses a known distributor brand to advertise the product where it is the middlemen or distributor brand policy marketing the product under a renowned middleman brand as this strategy is used by organisations without adequate finance for advertisement and promotion which can be an advantage to the producer in the market.

7.12.2 Positioning a Brand

Positioning a brand means occupying a unique place in the minds of the consumers (Saqib, 2020). The following are the various ways for positioning a brand:

■ Taking advantage of a trending situation
■ Connecting various users
■ Positioning according to consumer lifestyle
■ Advertising the benefits
■ Accruing a competitive position

- Benefits offered by the product
- Positioning a brand creates an image in the customers' minds, to which they can relate
- It increases the sales of the product

7.13 Brand Equity

Brand equity refers to the value an organisation enjoys from an engrained brand name (Keller & Brexendorf, 2019). A good brand is likely to offer more financial value as compared to a lesser known brand. Consumers hold the perception that a product with an established brand will be of better quality than the ones with less established brands. Hence, a well-branded product has better advantages over products not found in that light. Brand equity valuation is difficult and does not have any basic criteria. Some of the elements associated with it include consumer loyalty, awareness of the brand, quality of the product, association with the brand, and proprietary assets owned by the brand.

7.13.1 Brand Benefits

Brands have various advantages compared to unknown products. Some of the benefits are as follows:

- It increases customer confidence in purchasing decision.
- It increases the efficiency and effectiveness of advertisement and promotion.
- Brand loyalty is increased.
- Products can be priced higher for better margins and higher return on investment (ROI).
- Extension of brand.
- Leverage in trade.
- Unique position of the brand.

7.13.2 Packaging

Packaging is a method used to protect the product from external factors during transportation or storage (Vila-Lopez & Küster-Boluda, 2021).

Depending on the nature of the product, the packaging can differ. At the same time, packaging creates a first impression on the consumer so it should be designed accordingly. The reasons for packaging range from making the product attractive; promoting the identity of the product, product development, and sustainability of the product; and revealing the image and genuineness of the brand.

7.13.2.1 Packaging Strategies

The packaging design of a product can provide an advantage in the market over similar products in the same category. The following are the different strategies for effective packaging: packaging of product line, multiple packaging, and changing the package. Proper execution of packaging strategies can increase the attractiveness and durability of the product.

7.13.2.2 Labelling

Labelling is the process of marking an identity on the product. The information used for labelling contains details such as manufacturer's name and address, name and address of the distributor, maximum retail price (MRP) of the product, manufacturing date of the product, the method used to manufacture, ingredients used, precaution details, quantity, and expiry date. The information provided in labelling is important as it helps trace the origin and also determine the genuineness of the product.

7.13.2.3 Product Mix

Product mix denotes the set of products offered by an organisation. For instance, Reliance Industries has several products including cellular service, power, and entertainment. Hence, a strategy should be planned such that the uniqueness of the product can be established.

7.13.2.4 Positioning the Product

Positioning the product includes positioning in relation to competition; positioning by product attributes, uses, user, and benefits; and positioning in relation to the price and quality of other products in the segment.

7.13.2.5 Product Mix Expansion

It includes product depth and product line. These are the dimensions of the product mix. It depends on the number of products manufactured by an organisation.

7.13.2.6 Planned Obsolescence

Planned obsolescence is a strategy to create space for a new product with the help of advertisements showing an existing product to be out of date or fashion. This strategy is however considered controversial as it creates an unnecessary void that can be filled with a new product satisfying the thirst for newness. Planned obsolescence could be technological obsolescence or style obsolescence.

7.14 Conclusion

Marketing is the heartbeat of every organisation; hence, it requires keen attention. Most importantly, the market for the products of the organisation must be defined. The product must necessarily have a high demand potential. This would help with effective marketing strategy formulation and resource allocation. The marketing concept aims at satisfying the needs of the customer underpins the entire marketing process which espouses value offering. In the process of offering value to customers, the marketing plan entails that the marketing mix strategies must fall in sync. Competitive activity must also be analysed, so appropriate strategies are derived to manage the competition. Besides, the marketing environments must be monitored carefully to minimise any negative influence and maximise opportunities. Another significant part of marketing is branding, which clarifies the personality and uniqueness of the product and also helps with easy identification. All these strategies underscore the indispensable role marketing plays within an organisation.

Marketing in the post-COVID-19 period is now a combination of online and in-person transactions. Market is no longer restricted to a particular geographical area. Patrons of a product may choose to order online for the sellers to deliver to the address provided by the buyer.

Businesses have to strengthen their marketing departments. Businesses should realise that if they fail to digitalise their operations, they will be left behind and competitors will capture the market. The convenience of the buyer is paramount and customers are prepared to pay a little more to enjoy this convenience. In partnership with financial institutions and telcos, methods of payment such as scan and pay, bank transfer, and mobile money transfer have been deployed to make payment of goods and services easy. Once payment for a good is made, the services of delivery companies can be utilised to reach out to the clients who have made the payment.

References

Abba, M.T. (2021). Analysing competitor and creating a competitive advantage. *Interdisciplinary Journal of Applied and Basics Subjects*, 1(8), 31–42.

AbouElgheit, E. (2022). A 2020s marketing taxonomy for augmented reality customer experience. In: Rezaei, N. (ed.) *Transdisciplinarity. Integrated Science, Vol 5* 267–284. Springer, Cham.

Ancillai, C., Terho, H., Cardinali, S. & Pascucci, F. (2019). Advancing social media driven sales research: Establishing conceptual foundations for B-to-B social selling. *Industrial Marketing Management*, 82, 293–308.

Antika, F.P. (2023). Literature review: Factors affecting marketing strategy, market size, technology, and end users on market segmentation and competitive space. *The Eastasouth Management and Business*, 1(2), 37–43.

Barrachina Fernández, M., García-Centeno, M.D.C. & Calderón Patier, C. (2021). Women sustainable entrepreneurship: Review and research agenda. *Sustainability*, 13(21), 12047.

Basalamah, J., Syahnur, M.H., Ashoer, M. & Bahari, A.F. (2020). Consumer behavior in online transportation services: A systematic review of business strategies. *Ilomata International Journal of Management*, 1(3), 134–144.

Bassano, C., Barile, S., Piciocchi, P., Spohrer, J.C., Iandolo, F. & Fisk, R. (2019). Storytelling about places: Tourism marketing in the digital age. *Cities*, 87, 10–20.

Benzaghta, M.A., Elwalda, A., Mousa, M.M., Erkan, I. & Rahman, M. (2021). SWOT analysis applications: An integrative literature review. *Journal of Global Business Insights*, 6(1), 55–73.

Cartwright, S., Liu, H. & Raddats, C. (2021). Strategic use of social media within business-to-business (B2B) marketing: A systematic literature review. *Industrial Marketing Management*, 97, 35–58.

Cooper, R.G. (2019). The drivers of success in new-product development. *Industrial Marketing Management*, 76, 36–47.

Cortez, R.M., Clarke, A.H. & Freytag, P.V. (2021). B2B market segmentation: A systematic review and research agenda. *Journal of Business Research*, 126, 415–428.

Da Silva, A.L. & Castañeda-Ayarza, J.A. (2021). Macro-environment analysis of the corn ethanol fuel development in Brazil. *Renewable and Sustainable Energy Reviews*, 135, 110387.

Dellaert, B.G. (2019). The consumer production journey: Marketing to consumers as co-producers in the sharing economy. *Journal of the Academy of Marketing Science*, 47(2), 238–254.

Desai, V. & Vidyapeeth, B. (2019). Digital marketing: A review. *International Journal of Trend in Scientific Research and Development*, 5(5), 196–200.

Fauzi, D.H.F. & Ali, H. (2021). Determination of purchase and repurchase decisions: Product quality and price analysis (case study on Samsung smartphone consumers in the City of Jakarta). *Dinasti International Journal of Digital Business Management*, 2(5), 794–810.

Fisher, N.I. & Kordupleski, R.E. (2019). Good and bad market research: A critical review of net promoter score. *Applied Stochastic Models in Business and Industry*, 35(1), 138–151.

Hao, A.W., Paul, J., Trott, S., Guo, C. & Wu, H.H. (2021). Two decades of research on nation branding: A review and future research agenda. *International Marketing Review*, 38(1), 46–69.

Igor Ansoff, H. (1986). Competitive strategy analysis on the personal computer. *Journal of Business Strategy*, 6(3), 28–36.

Kang, J., Diao, Z. & Zanini, M.T. (2021). Business-to-business marketing responses to COVID-19 crisis: A business process perspective. *Marketing Intelligence and Planning*, 39(3), 454–468.

Karagiannopoulos, G.D., Georgopoulos, N. & Nikolopoulos, K. (2005). Fathoming Porter's five forces model in the internet era. *info*, 7(6), 66–76.

Katsikeas, C., Leonidou, L. & Zeriti, A. (2020). Revisiting international marketing strategy in a digital era: Opportunities, challenges, and research directions. *International Marketing Review*, 37(3), 405–424.

Keller, K.L. & Brexendorf, T.O. (2019). Measuring brand equity. In: Esch, F.R. (ed.) *Handbuch Markenführung. Springer Reference Wirtschaft*(pp. 1409–1439). Springer Gabler, Wiesbaden.

Kim, W. (2019). A practical guide for understanding online business models. *International Journal of Web Information Systems*, 15(1), 71–82.

Kim, Y.K. & Sullivan, P. (2019). Emotional branding speaks to consumers' heart: The case of fashion brands. *Fashion and Textiles*, 6(1), 1–16.

Kumar, B. & Sharma, A. (2022). Examining the research on social media in business-to-business marketing with a focus on sales and the selling process. *Industrial Marketing Management*, 102, 122–140.

Kumar, S. (2022). Critical assessment of green financing initiatives in emerging market: A review of India Green bond issuances. *Academy of Marketing Studies Journal*, 26(5), 1–14.

Lahtinen, V., Dietrich, T. & Rundle-Thiele, S. (2020). Long live the marketing mix: Testing the effectiveness of the commercial marketing mix in a social marketing context. *Journal of Social Marketing*, 10(3), 357–375.

Lee, N.R. & Kotler, P. (2019). *Social marketing: Behavior change for social good.* Sage Publications.

Leng, J., Ruan, G., Jiang, P., Xu, K., Liu, Q., Zhou, X. & Liu, C. (2020). Blockchain-empowered sustainable manufacturing and product lifecycle management in industry 4.0: A survey. *Renewable and Sustainable Energy Reviews*, 132, 110112.

Lin, J.S.C. & Chang, Y.C. (2012). Retailers' new product acceptance decisions: Incorporating the buyer-supplier relationship perspective. *Journal of Business and Industrial Marketing*, 27(2), 89–99.

Mansaray, H.E. (2019). Relating marketing and corporate strategy-an overview. *International Journal of Innovative Studies in Sciences and Engineering Technology*, 5(11), 24–32.

Mintz, O., Gilbride, T.J., Lenk, P. & Currim, I.S. (2021). The right metrics for marketing-mix decisions. *International Journal of Research in Marketing*, 38(1), 32–49.

Ngugi, D.G., Mcharo, M. & Munge, M. (2020). Application of the 4 Ps marketing mix by micro and small-scale traders in Kenya: Impact on household incomes. *Journal of Applied Economic Sciences*, 15(3), 654–664.

Nikbin, D., Iranmanesh, M., Ghobakhloo, M. & Foroughi, B. (2022). Marketing mix strategies during and after COVID-19 pandemic and recession: A systematic review. *Asia-Pacific Journal of Business Administration*, 14(4), 405–420.

Nunan, D., Malhotra, N.K. & Birks, D.F. (2020). *Marketing research.* Pearson UK.

Othman, B., Harun, A., Rashid, W., Nazeer, S., Kassim, A. & Kadhim, K. (2019). The influences of service marketing mix on customer loyalty towards Umrah travel agents: Evidence from Malaysia. *Management Science Letters*, 9(6), 865–876.

Pal, S. (2019). Understanding the impact of marketing transformation on sales and marketing alignment. *Journal of Brand Strategy*, 8(1), 48–57.

Palav, M.R. & Jagtap, S.D. (2020). Research in marketing audit a systematic literature review. *PARIDNYA-The MIBM Research Journal*, 7(1), 1–25.

Pimenta da Gama, A. (2020). How good is the marketing method? Measuring the process and the outcomes. *Journal of Business Strategy*, 41(6), 57–67.

Porter, M.E. (1997). Competitive strategy. *Measuring Business Excellence*, 1(2), 12–17.

Ren, S., Chan, H.L. & Siqin, T. (2020). Demand forecasting in retail operations for fashionable products: Methods, practices, and real case study. *Annals of Operations Research*, 291(1–2), 761–777.

Riyadi, A. & Rangkuti, S. (2016). The influence of marketing mix and customer purchasing decision process on customer satisfaction. In *Asia tourism forum 2016-the 12th Biennial conference of hospitality and tourism industry in Asia* (pp. 528–534). Atlantis Press.

Saqib, N. (2020). Positioning – a literature review. *PSU Research Review*, 5(2), 141–169.

Shabbir, M.S. & Wisdom, O. (2020). The relationship between corporate social responsibility, environmental investments and financial performance: Evidence from manufacturing companies. *Environmental Science and Pollution Research*, 27(32), 39946–39957.

Sheth, J. (2021). New areas of research in marketing strategy, consumer behavior, and marketing analytics: The future is bright. *Journal of Marketing Theory and Practice*, 29(1), 3–12.

Song, M., Wang, S. & Zhang, H. (2020). Could environmental regulation and R&D tax incentives affect green product innovation? *Journal of Cleaner Production*, 258, 120849.

Stocchi, L., Pourazad, N., Michaelidou, N., Tanusondjaja, A. & Harrigan, P. (2021). Marketing research on mobile apps: Past, present and future. *Journal of the Academy of Marketing Science*, 50–(1), 195–225.

Tran, N.L. & Rudolf, W. (2022). Social media and destination branding in tourism: A systematic review of the literature. *Sustainability*, 14(20), 13528.

Umboh, I.A. & Aryanto, V.D.W. (2019). Improving export marketing performance: A conceptual model of adaptation marketing strategy. *Calitatea*, 20(171), 62–69.

Varadarajan, R. (2020). Customer information resources advantage, marketing strategy and business performance: A market resources based view. *Industrial Marketing Management*, 89, 89–97.

Vila-Lopez, N. & Küster-Boluda, I. (2021). A bibliometric analysis on packaging research: Towards sustainable and healthy packages. *British Food Journal*, 123(2), 684–701.

Wang, L., Liu, Z., Liu, A. & Tao, F. (2021). Artificial intelligence in product life-cycle management. *The International Journal of Advanced Manufacturing Technology*, 114(3–4), 771–796.

Zhang, Q., Lu, X., Peng, Z. & Ren, M. (2019). Perspective: A review of lifecycle management research on complex products in smart-connected environments. *International Journal of Production Research*, 57(21), 6758–6779.

Case Study

Market Research Companies Run Out of Information

A ready supply of information about customers, actual and potential, is vital to marketing managers. Consumers have become increasingly fragmented and sophisticated in their buying habits, while the growth in the size of business units calls for information which can be easily analysed and acted upon. Gone are the days when most market research could be done simply by the owner/manager of a business listening to their customers.

Specialist data collection companies have come to play an important role in the task of collecting information about buyers. Organisations such as Experian, CACI, and Claritas have developed a role in providing socioeconomic and lifestyle data which are sold to client companies to make their targeting more effective. With the growth in direct marketing, it is important for many clients to have specific information about each individual customer, rather than a general aggregate for the whole market. This applies to information about new prospects, as well as new and additional information from people already on their databases, which is important because people's circumstances change. In contrast to client firms' need for this information, consumers, by the end of the 1990s, were showing increasing resistance to providing information for commercial purposes.

The market research industry has been concerned for a number of years about falling response rates to quantitative surveys. A Market Research Society report of 1997 pointed out that the public rarely distinguishes between anonymous research, database building, or telephone calls that start off asking for information but end up with a hard sell. A report prepared in 1998 by the Future Foundation identified that only 50 per cent of consumers were happy to provide personal information to firms with which they deal, down from over 60 per cent in 1995. A core of people surveyed appeared to be not interested in taking part in data collection exercises at all and won't fill in questionnaires. The 2001 UK Census of Population – a foundation for many research exercises – appears to have fallen short of its claim to be a universal survey of the entire UK population, with reports of up to 2 million "missing" people. For marketers, this is a worrying development. If the public does not offer information about their needs, wants, attitudes, and behaviour, it makes the life of the marketer more difficult.

There are a number of factors that may explain this trend. The first is that many more companies are now seeking to obtain information from buyers. Globally, ESOMAR's monitoring of the industry shows that the total market for market research worldwide in 2001 was US$ 15,890 million, with the United States accounting for 39 per cent of this total and the EU 37 per cent. The Market Research Society estimated that in 2000, the size of the UK Market Research Industry was £955 million, with one of the biggest growth areas being opinion research about social or moral issues. In addition, direct marketing companies have been building marketing databases of their own customers. Saturation appeared to be setting in. The result is that we can hardly visit a restaurant, buy a new item of electrical equipment, or take an aeroplane journey without being invited to give our comments. Sometimes we are approached unsolicited for our views, whether in the street or by telephone. Information is a key element of a firm's competitive advantage, so they are putting more and more effort into collecting information about customers.

Second, consumers are becoming increasingly aware that information that only they can reveal about themselves has commercial value. Research from the Future Foundation suggested that the majority of people were happy to provide personal details if the result was better products or services. However, the public's experience of how well these data are used often falls short of their expectations in terms of how it benefits them personally.

But with so much information gathering going on, is there a danger of "survey fatigue" setting in? Just how many times can a company ask customers questions about what they think of the company before the whole process of carrying out a survey becomes an irritation in itself? Do customers think that their comments will ever be taken notice of by management? Careful organisation of surveys can improve response rates. Stopping people when they are in a hurry to catch a train will not make an interviewer popular, but approaching them when they are captive with nothing else to do (e.g., waiting for baggage at an airport following a flight) may be more successful.

Developing some form of meaningful relationship with a recipient prior to receiving a questionnaire seems to be important. At its simplest level, an individual would receive a very simple first form. If they complete and return this, it is followed a couple of months later with a reward pack of money off vouchers and samples, plus a second, more detailed questionnaire. As an example, research by Air Miles concluded that the company gets much better, more robust data if it saves detailed questions until members have had some experience with its services, rather than asking detailed questions of new recruits. And drinks retailer Bottoms Up was able to persuade 10,000 members of its loyalty programme, the Imbibers Club, to agree to telephone interviews on their drinking habits, something that would be very difficult to do out of the blue.

A more sophisticated approach is used by Consodata, which has a contract to collect, manage, and analyse household data for the "Jigsaw" Consumer Needs Consortium (Kimberly-Clark, Unilever, and Cadbury Schweppes). The chosen vehicle is a magazine with special offers, which over time is tailored to the individual needs of respondents as more is learnt about them. As an incentive, everybody gets a reward, instead of being offered a minuscule chance of winning a jackpot. Industry sources suggested that the response rate to the first issue of the Jigsaw consortium's magazine was 30–35 per cent, in line with the results sometimes claimed for similar, data-collecting surveys undertaken via customer magazines. Again, the point is clear that consumers are freer with their information when dealing with organisations they already know and trust.

Bigger bribes to encourage people to provide data are part of the researcher's armoury. This ploy has reached new heights in the United States with reports of home shopping companies offering free computers and internet access in return for household data and the acceptance of advertising on their screen. But large bribes can lead to another problem of samples being biased towards a new breed of professional market research respondents. There have been reports that focus groups are increasingly being dominated by a small circle of individuals who can make a reasonable living off the fee paid to participants. For research companies, such people may be readily available and need less training and instruction than a novice. But is the information that they yield of any great value?

Adapted from "Data Firm React to Survey Fatigue," *Marketing*, April 29, 1999, pp. 29–30.

Case Study Review Questions

1. Suggest additional methods which companies can use to improve the effectiveness of their consumer data collection. What examples have you encountered?

2. Discuss the limitations of statistically based consumer databases of the type discussed. Do qualitative approaches based on small groups offer any advantages?

3. What effects do you expect the development of interactive electronic media will have on the collection of marketing research information from consumers?

Chapter 8

Accounting and Financial Statements

Learning Outcomes

At the end of this chapter, you will be able to:

- explain the nature and reasons for accounting and bookkeeping.
- explain accounting ratios and terminologies.
- distinguish between financial and management accounting.
- interpret financial, income statements, profit and revenue, or income statements.

Chapter Outline

- Introduction
- The Nature of Accounting
- Accounting Ratios
- Conclusion
- References
- Case Study and Case Study Questions

8.1 Introduction

In organised societies, we find goods and other valuables held by individuals, groups, and institutions in trust for others. The purpose for holding

DOI: 10.4324/9781003458524-8

such goods and valuables could be for safekeeping (for example, gold or jewellery deposited at the bank) or with the intention that the goods or valuables should be used in a manner that yields returns for the owner(s). For instance, board of directors have been entrusted with the cash of shareholders, and they are to ensure that the cash yields maximum returns for the shareholders. Local and central governments also mobilise revenue through taxes and taxpayers expect that the revenues will be used for the benefit of society. The shareholders, donor agencies, and taxpayers, among others who hand over monies to others, expect feedback on how these monies are being used. Even the sole proprietor who single-handedly invests money in a business needs feedback on how the money is being used to ascertain the business' financial performance. Consequently, accounting and financial management have become a topic of importance to businesses and non-profit-making entities alike. However, this chapter focuses on businesses.

Accounting and finance are of utmost importance to businesses. They determine the business' success and its existence to some extent. For instance, poor keeping of accounting records tends to cause liquidity and cash flow issues in the business (Habib et al., 2020). Accounting and finance are practically used by businesses to ensure the judicious use of financial resources. Consequently, the subject is of importance to all businesses irrespective of size and legal form of ownership. Aside profit-seeking ventures, non-profit-seeking ones such as charities, government, and non-governmental organisations also apply financial accounting concepts to exhibit to stakeholders that the finances gathered are being used in the best way to achieve stated aims and objectives (Agyemang, O'Dwyer & Unerman, 2019).

This chapter explores the nature of accounting, bookkeeping, the basic terminology in accounting and finance, the purpose and uses of accounting information, and the types of financial statements. The chapter further discusses the key financial reports with accounting information shared with its users.

8.2 The Nature of Accounting

Accounting is a process related to the identification, organisation, classification, recording, summarisation, and communication of information related usually to economic activities (Jackson, 2022). Better still, accounting comprises recording, measurement, and interpretation of financial information needed for business decision-making. The accounting function is often carried out by accountants who may be private or public accountants. On one hand, certified public accountants (CPAs) are state-certified individuals who provide accounting services such as preparing financial accounts and the filing of tax returns to intricate audits of corporate financial accounts (Deno, 2019). On the other hand, private accountants have titles such as tax accountants, internal auditors, and the like. They are usually involved in several of the most critical financial decisions of the firms they work with.

In Ghana, the need for accounting and financial reporting is espoused by the Companies Code 1963 now the Companies' Act 2019 (Act 992). The Act (Companies Code 1963) specifies the need for the preparation and publication of financial statements. However, it is silent on the accounting standards that should be used (Appiah-Konadu, Apetorgbor & Atanya, 2022). Hence, the de facto standards presented by the Institute of Chartered Accountants, Ghana (ICAG), are adopted by corporate bodies.

The 1990s saw the ICAG issuing the Ghana National Accounting Standards. In 2007, the institute also adopted International Financial Reporting Standards (IFRS) as the requisite accounting standard for the preparation of financial statements of all insurance firms, state enterprises, banks, pension funds, brokers of securities, and public utility companies (Tawiah, 2019). In 2010, the IFRS was adopted by the institute for Small and Medium Scale Enterprises (SMEs). These standards were applied in 2015 with an accompanying guide to enable typical micro-enterprises to apply the IFRS (Imhanzenobe, 2022). Other businesses are, however, allowed to adopt full IFRS or IFRS for SMEs.

Accounting and bookkeeping are sometimes used interchangeably, albeit, the two concepts are entirely different. Accounting is considered to include bookkeeping and is wider than bookkeeping (Stauffer & Takahashi, 2023). To help distinguish between accounting and bookkeeping, the former can be thought of as a process of transforming raw data documented in bookkeeping into valuable information. It is therefore right to say that bookkeeping is an input to accounting activity. Bookkeeping, typically, relates to the recording of the day-to-day financial activities of a business. Data in themselves make no definite meaning until they have been processed to create meaning (Ranatarisza et al., 2022). For instance, it is not enough if stakeholders of a business get to know how much the items they sell cost; for instance, a gallon of honey costs GH₵ 200. This is not enough to help the business or its stakeholders in decision-making. Data like that will only become relevant information when it is combined with other data to create a complete meaning. In this context, the business and its stakeholders may need other data such as how much profit the business made after selling to the customer or the cost of the gallon of honey the business owner bought from another supplier, among others. Whereas the accounting function is performed by accountants, the bookkeeping function is undertaken by bookkeepers (Rogosic, 2019).

Further, there is a communication facet of accounting. This involves reporting the information acquired by a business in the accounting process to concerned parties, like managers of the business and owners (Abad-Segura & González-Zamar, 2020). Details of business dealings over a specified period must be monitored for summarisation, presentation, and interpretation. This makes it possible for an assessment of a business' financial position and performance at a specified date. The accounting period is the length of time covered by the data of a financial statement. Others also term it "period of account." This accounting period could cover any period, say quarterly (every three months), semi-annually (every six months), and yearly (every twelve months). However, this length of time is influenced by the purpose for which the accounting results are intended, like providing management with accounting information to support a bank loan application (Al-Hashimy, 2022). Businesses commonly go by the yearly accounting period and present yearly results needed for certain purposes including taxation or filing with a regulatory body. Conversely, only specific situations require accounting information prepared for lengths of time apart from the year. The end date of accounting periods is known as the business' "closing date" or "accounting reference date" (Geng & Kalargiros, 2022). For firms in Ghana, this closing date can be any date aside from the calendar year based on preferences, although this might not be the same in other jurisdictions.

As stated earlier, accounting information provides managers with information that is necessary to monitor and control business activities and also for decision-making. The information provided via accounting is future-oriented than focusing on past transactions. This adds a management dimension to accounting as part of the broader management information system (MIS) of an organisation (Alawamleh et al., 2021). Given this, accounting is occasionally referred to as "accounting information system (AIS) or simply "accounting system." Be mindful that typically, as the bookkeeper records data in the books of the business, the accountant has to translate the data into useful information for some purposes. The relevance of accounting information is based on its value, timeliness, completeness, and quality (El-Ebiary et al., 2023). These stated characteristics of useful accounting information can be achieved if the data have been properly recorded.

8.2.1 Bookkeeping

The term bookkeeping refers to the process of recording the daily transactions of a business in its financial records (Bellucci, Cesa Bianchi & Manetti, 2022). In bookkeeping, recorded transactions need to be prior classified such that comparable transactions can be captured in the same account. For instance, a business records transactions relating to purchases of goods and services as well as sales in different accounts according to their nature. Typically, records that detail similar transactions are recorded in either a ledger or a book. One or a few pages are then devoted to a particular transaction like sales of certain products. In view of this, records are usually communally termed the "books" of a business (Maddox, 2022; Elliott & Elliott, 2007).

The act of bookkeeping is not new and dates back several hundreds or even thousands of years. The need for bookkeeping erupted because business owners needed to keep track of creditors (institutions or people who owe them money) and debtors (institutions or people they owe money) (Hin, 2019). This was to enable them to determine the financial standing of the business. In earlier years, bookkeeping was done based on common sense. That is, data the business owners considered necessary were the ones recorded. Bookkeeping does not only denote the recording of transactions as explained but is also repeatedly used as a truncation for double-entry bookkeeping, a system invented by Fra Luca Bartolomeo de Pacioli, an Italian mathematician (considered the father of accounting and bookkeeping) (Mert, 2022). Till today, it remains the utmost prevalent technique of bookkeeping. The "books" containing the records of the business transactions are to be maintained and kept up to date by the bookkeeper. To achieve this, transactions are recorded in a logical and timely manner. The recording of the transaction could be recorded chronologically as they happen or treated like items in batches. Also, recording of transactions could be done through electronic means (computerised bookkeeping), which is the commonly used means in modern times, or manually in books or on paper (Topor et al., 2021).

The act of recording transactions into individual accounts is known as "postings." In this era where most accounting activities are computerised, a computer program can ensure the quick and accurate posting of financial transactions if the data have been correctly entered. The posting of transactions to single accounts allows individual accountants to exhibit a trail of transactions that have taken place to facilitate tracking and sales monitoring of specific items overtime. The existence of accounts allows a business to develop a formal report to indicate the financial standing of the business. The monetary transactions entered can be totalled to give a better view of an issue of interest. For illustration, the entire sales of a product or service in a given period can be determined. The totalling of the single accounts may also bring to light that one side of the double-entry account surpasses the other in value and helps determine the balance. The balances for the individual accounts are then listed in a financial statement called the "trial balance." Balancing off separate accounts and preparing the trial balance is vital in determining the profit or loss made by the business (Bellucci et al., 2022).

8.2.2 Accounting Terminologies

There are specific names for various parts of financial statements. These came about in response to different customs, rules, and regulations of accounting bodies such as the International Accounting Standards Board (IASB) and the introduction of International Financial Reporting Standards (IFRSs) and International Accounting Standards (IASs) (Maru, 2022). For example, for several years, the "profit and loss account" was a usual term but was perceived as inaccurate, especially when applied by entities that are not-for-profit-making. As such, the international accounting standards (IASs 1), which oversees the presentation of financial statements, announced the term "income statement" which has universal applicability. The IAS 1 also suggested that the term "statement of financial position" should be used instead of "balance sheet" (Imhanzenobe, 2022). However, the adoption of this new term (statement of financial position) is not mandatory. Again, "income statements" has been widely used and embraced but the case is different with the use of "statement of financial position." In recent times, whereas more accounting training manuals use the term "statement of financial position," several businesses still use the term "balance sheet" (Deno, 2019). Aside from the extensive application of the term "balance sheet," it is equally useful in accounting studies where it reminds students to keep the balance sheet "balanced," meaning the account should have the same total figure on both sides.

In the study and practice of accounting, the student or practitioner must understand some basic accounting terms. Below are some basic accounting terms for readers' perusal.

1. **Assets**

In the context of a business, assets refer to the wealth which has been accumulated by the business. Assets are owned by the organisation without the attachment to any loan. Assets could be tangible or intangible (Jiang, 2022). Examples of tangible assets are cash, inventory, buildings, machinery, accounts receivable, fixtures, and equipment, among others. Intangible assets cover goodwill, brand equity, and others. Assets may also be objects that depreciate as time goes by or goods that are sold to customers.

2. **Revenue**

Revenue relates to the total amount of all income made by a business or organisation at any point in time (Sundaram, Sharma & Shakya, 2020). Revenue and income are often used interchangeably. Revenue may be gathered from cash sales, subscription fees, credit sales, interests charged, and others. It however diverges from receipts as it even covers monies that the business has not collected yet at the time of the delivery of the goods or service.

3. **Trade Discount**

Trade discount describes a monotonous reduction of the price of an item or product (Stojković & Jeremijev, 2021). It is the percentage discounted from the selling price, and it is often based on the volume of goods ordered at a point in time. As a practice, customers who buy huge volumes of items from the seller are likely to gain higher discounts, and customers who buy lesser get lesser discounts.

4. **Balance Sheet**

It is one of the basic financial statements vital to financial accounting. It depicts the total assets of a business and the source of financing for the assets, as in debt or equity financing (Abrohms & Schuler, 2019). The balance sheet is also called a "statement of net worth" or "statement of financial position" as it helps determine the financial health of a business. It is based on the basic equation: Assets = Liabilities + Equity.

5. **General Ledger**

The general ledger refers to the aspect of the bookkeeping ledger that contains the income statement, trial balance, balance sheet, and others (Shahrina et al., 2022). In the general ledger, business transactions such as sales, expenses, credit purchases, and others are documented. The general ledger contains all of the information necessary to prepare financial statements.

6. **Gross Margin**

Gross margin refers to the total amount received through sales, minus related costs like manufacturing costs, material costs, supplies, and wholesale costs (Munna, 2021).

7. **Loss**

When a business' expenses exceed its revenue, then it is said to have made a loss. Better still, making a loss represents a situation where a good or service is sold lesser than the cost of manufacture or supply.

8. **On Credit/On account**

On credit or account implies that a business' item or product has been sold to a customer or buyer on a credit basis. In this situation, payment is not made immediately to the business but at a later date. On credit or account sales may result in interest charges.

9. **Receipts**

In accounting terms, receipts are the overall amount of money (cash) a business makes from business transactions in a day. Receipts are limited to the sales the business makes daily and does not include other revenues.

10. **Trial Balance**

A trial balance constitutes the presentation of all ledger balances in a single worksheet at a particular date. It includes both debits and credits for an account. Entries in the trial balance must balance, meaning that entries at both the credit and debit sides should tally to the same amount. In the trial balance, the lists of balances in the accounts of the organisation's general ledger are shown. Accounts with zero balances are however not represented in the trial balance.

11. Accounting Period

An accounting period is in reference to the span of time that the information on financial statements covers. It also communicates the period utilised to determine the accounting performance of the business. Accounting periods often cover one year (yearly), six months (semi-annually), three months (quarterly), or one month (monthly). Accounting periods are needed by investors to compare the results of successive periods.

12. Accounts Payable (Sundry Creditors)

Accounts payable are short-term financial responsibilities an organisation holds towards another through the purchase of goods or services. In other words, it is money owed by an organisation to its creditors.

13. Accounts Receivable (Sundry Debtors)

Accounts receivables refer to monies that are to be collected by a business from its debtors or customers. They are amounts owed by a business' customers for the purchase of goods and/or services.

14. Current Assets

Current assets are items that are owned by an organisation and can easily be turned into cash in the business' standard operational cycle, which often spans one year. Examples are inventory, debtors, and deposits, among others.

15. Fixed Assets

Fixed assets are the properties of a business that are not anticipated to be changed into cash. They are used to generate revenue for the business.

16. **Expenses**

The costs that a business incurs in its productions and operations constitute its expense. Expenses are the cost of operations that a business makes to generate revenue. This echoes the popular saying that "it costs money to make money." The common expenses a business makes cover employee wages, inventory, leases, and utilities, among others.

17. **Gross Profit**

Gross profit represents the variance in the cost incurred in getting goods and the actual sales made. In essence, the gross profit is the total sales made by the firm, less the actual cost of the goods sold.

18. **Inventory (Stock)**

Inventory refers to goods purchased or manufactured by a business, which is anticipated to be sold to customers soon. It is also known as merchandise. The main purpose of inventory in a business is to be sold to customers for a profit and nothing else.

19. **Stock Turnover**

Stock turnover relates to the average number of times an organisation sells and changes its inventory in a given period. The determination of inventory turnover helps businesses in better decision-making concerning manufacturing, pricing, marketing, and purchasing inventory.

20. **Net Profit**

Net profit is how much money a business makes after the cost of goods as well as operating expenses have been subtracted from the sales revenue.

21. **Liabilities**

The liabilities of an organisation refer to the amount it owes other external organisations.

22. **Long-Term Liabilities**

Long-term liabilities are the amounts of monies a business owes other entities, of which the due time for repayment extends beyond 12 months.

23. **Liquidity**

The term liquidity describes how easily a business can convert assets into cash. Assets such as inventory and bonds are considered very liquid. This is because, even within days, these inventories and bonds can be converted into cash. On the contrary, fixed assets like plants, equipment, property, and others cannot easily be converted into cash. As such, they are not considered liquid. Liquidity denotes the position of an organisation to pay its financial obligations as they become due.

8.2.3 Reasons for Accounting

The provision of financial information to managers, business owners, and other stakeholders is the main aim of accounting (Hassan & Marston, 2019). These financial data meet diverse objectives including stewardship, planning and control, accountability, and decision-making. These are discussed in subsequent sections.

8.2.3.1 Stewardship

Normally, the people who manage or run a business are not the owners, especially with large organisations. Other people often invest monies in businesses and employ other people to run them. These hired people manage the money and resources of the set-up businesses. They, therefore, play the role of stewards for the owners or principals of the organisations. The agency concept makes it obligatory for managers to make financial data available to the principals. The agents do not own the resources of the business but control them (O'Connell & Ward, 2020). Figure 8.1 depicts the ideology of stewardship. The arrows in the figure indicate the movement of resources, chains of responsibility, and information flow. Ideology of Stewardship

8.2.3.2 Accountability

The idea of accountability, though similar to stewardship, is wider as it covers other stakeholders of the business such as the public, employees, and others, other than owners/shareholders. It is expected of stewards or agents of

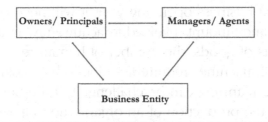

Figure 8.1 Stewardship

businesses to give accounts of how they have managed the resources of the business in a given period. The duty of accountability is demonstrated by the provision of financial data comprising a balance sheet and income statement (Rodríguez-Fernández, Gaspar-González & Sánchez-Teba, 2020). Accountability goes beyond the idea of accounting and how the resources of a business have been used to cover the notion of acting responsibly and being ready to face the consequences of irresponsible and unwarrantable actions.

8.2.3.3 Control

Control is another use or purpose of accounting information. The managers of a business need to observe and track the activities and operations of the business to determine if the business is operating according to plan. If any deviations are detected, then corrective measures will need to be undertaken where viable. The regular provision of accounting information is useful for control purposes. From the point of view of the classic agency perspective, the separation of corporate managers from external investors can birth inherent conflict. Corporate control measures are thus the means through which managers of businesses are made to act in the interest of investors and not pursue self-interest (Alabdullah & Maryanti, 2021). Control mechanisms could be internal or external. On the one hand, internal control mechanisms include plans for managerial incentives, internal labour market, and director monitoring. On the other hand, external control instruments include external managerial labour market, security laws that protect external investors against expropriation by internal stakeholders of the business, and external managerial labour market, among others.

8.2.3.4 Planning and Decision-Making

The acquisition of financial data enables business administrators to plan the future activities and operations of a business (Roychowdhury, Shroff & Verdi, 2019). For example, if a business plans to produce a certain number of units of goods in the next business operating year, it will need to have an idea about the quantity and amount involved to acquire raw materials to make that number of units of goods, the number of human resources required, the number and type of machines required, and all other costs involved in production. In practice, planning can be challenging if the business is seeking to enhance or reduce the production of an organisation's goods. It is even more problematic when the business needs to plan on producing new goods.

8.2.3.5 Financial and Management Accounting: Finding the Difference

In previous sections, the purposes for accounting have been espoused. This makes it evident that accounting information has different uses. It is therefore imperative to highlight various areas of accounting such as management and financial accounting, which forms the basis for the acquisition of accounting information (Pelz, 2019). Specific records will not be necessary for each of these except the information acquired from the records are organised, classified, summarised, and communicated into information that fits the different perspectives of accounting and the needs of users (Wolf et al., 2020). The differences between financial and management information are thence depicted below:

8.2.3.6 Financial Statements

The outcome of the accounting procedure is a number of financial statements. The most common types of financial statements are the cash flow statement, the balance sheet, and the income statement (Jackson, 2022; Edwards, 2013). These financial statements are provided to stockholders and the business' prospective investors in the annual report of the firm. The financial statements in view are also made available to other relevant actors, external to the firm such as creditors, internal revenue authority, government agencies, and others. Description of the financial statements mentioned above is presented in subsequent sections.

8.2.3.7 Income Statement

An income statement, also known as an operating statement or profit and loss (P&L) statement, is an abridged financial statement that demonstrates the financial performance of a business including revenue or the total profit or

Table 8.1 Financial and Management Accounting: Finding the Difference

Criteria	Financial accounting	Management accounting
Main purpose	Produces concise balance sheets and income statements by business managers. These financial statements are formal reports on their stewardship role in overseeing the resources of the business. Financial statements of public companies help stakeholders also make decisions. The financial information may be made public subject to the nature and ownership structure of the business.	This is about the use of recent and detailed information by stewards of businesses for planning and controlling business activities. The information provided here is not made available publicly but internally to the business providing it.
When information is prepared	Annually at the close of the accounting period. However, in view of the type of business entity in question, the financial information can be prepared every three months or six months.	Prepared monthly.
Governed by	Often mandatory and backed by law. It also follows required accounting or conventional accounting regulations.	Subject to the needs of management without legally having to produce anything in a specific format or produce at all.
Perspective	Information on previous performance, and may be out-of-date at the time of summarising the documents.	Comparative and current. Provides results for a specific month' together with the total for all months as well as comparative values for the year before.

Table created by authors

loss a business makes over a while (Jackson, 2022; Libby et al., 2004). The income is frequently derived from the sales of a firm's goods and services which are initially recorded in the individual accounts on the trial balance. The entries in the trial balance are then added up for use in the income statement. The income statement is also referred to as operating system.

The income generated from the sales as indicated in the income statement (Table 8.2) could also be referred to as sales turnover, sale revenue,

Table 8.2 Sample Income Statement Mr. Adofo and Sons – Income Statement for the Year Ended March 31, 2018

	GH₵	GH₵
Sales		40,000
Less: Cost of goods sold		
Opening inventory	14,000	
Purchases	22,000	
Total	36,000	
Less: Closing inventory	(12,000)	
		(24,000)
Gross profit		16,000
Less: Expenses		
Rent	3,000	
Lighting and heating expenses	2,800	
General expenses	800	
		(6,600)
Net profit		19,400

Table created by authors

turnover, or revenue. Income could be obtained through means other than sales. For instance, a business could gain income from a bank account in the form of bank interest. This is also added to the income statement. However, income from this will appear separately from the income made from sales. It could be captured as "bank interest receivable" or anything similar. A general term like "revenue" could be used to cover all kinds of income generated. There are no definite rules as to when "revenue" and "income" should be used; they are both commonly used terms in the accounting field. In a firm's efforts to produce and deliver services, the firm will have to use its resources, usually money. In the income statement, the full costs are deducted from the full revenue and the balance is then termed a profit or a loss. If the full income exceeds the full cost, then the result is a profit, otherwise known as surplus if the organisation is not profit oriented. On the contrary, the organisation makes a loss or deficit (for not-for-profit organisations) if the total income is less than the total costs. The organisation, classification, and presentation of revenue, and expense this way, make them meaningful information. It becomes possible to determine the financial performance of the business by calculating the profit or loss it makes. Take note that the accounting convention applied here puts figures to be deducted in brackets. This is most widely used in several countries.

8.2.3.8 The Balance Sheet

The balance sheet indicates the assets and liabilities of an organisation (Jackson, 2022). These assets and liabilities are listed from separate accounts on the trial balance and like items added together at the end of every accounting period. In accounting, the horizontal format and the vertical format are the two main methods used in displaying the assets and liabilities on a balance sheet. Using the horizontal format, all assets are listed on the left-hand side, and liabilities are listed on the right-hand side of the balance sheet. In line with the rules regarding double-entry bookkeeping, the total of the assets should equal the total of the liabilities. This is why this financial statement is called the "balance sheet"; both sides should add up to the same amount.

With the vertical format, capital is shown on the "bottom" half, and the "top" half displays assets with liabilities deducted from them. For example, current liabilities are deducted from current assets to give current net assets or liabilities. This is often referred to as the net assets approach.

In theory, any entity can produce a balance sheet using either format as it is just a matter of presentation.

8.3 Accounting Ratios

Accounting ratios are a collection of metrics that are applied in measuring the efficiency and profitability of a business on the basis of existing financial information or reports (Sanad & Al-Sartawi, 2021). Accounting ratios provide a means through which a business expresses the relationship between accounting data in terms of amount. They are also known as financial ratios. For example, a business' inventory turnover can be obtained by dividing its cost of goods sold for a stated year by the average inventory during that same year. This signifies the inventory turnover ratio. Accounting ratios are used for ratio analysis. These are calculations that measure the financial health of an organisation. Ratio analysis also makes complex information in financial statements such as the balance sheet and income statement into simple information that managers, lenders, owners, and other stakeholders

**Table 8.3 Sample Balance Sheet: Horizontal Format Mr. Adofo and Sons –
Balance Sheet for the Year Ended March 31, 2018**

	GH₵		GH₵
Non-current assets		Capital	
Fixtures and fittings	18,000	Cash introduced	25,000
		Retained earnings	11,000
Current assets		Net profit for the year	9,400
Inventory	12,000		
Trade receivables	5,800	Current liabilities	
Cash at bank and in hand	2,300	Trade payables	8,200
Drawings	15,500		
	53,600		53,600

Table created by authors

of a business can use to measure and compare the organisation's profitability, productivity, and others with other related organisations (Jackson, 2022). A "ratio" itself is a number divided by another, and the results of which show the relationship between the numbers. A ratio is a mathematical expression linking one number to another, frequently providing a relative comparison. Ratios in themselves are not very useful, but the relationship is determined by them. Hence, financial ratios are used to evaluate the performance of a firm. Financial ratios can be categorised into the following: profitability ratios, liquidity ratios, debt utilisation ratios, and asset utilisation ratios. These are discussed below.

8.3.1 *Profitability Ratios*

Profitability ratios are used in measuring how much net income a business has been able to generate in relation to its assets, sales, and owner's equity. Profitability ratios focus on the ability of the business to gain a return on investment in inventory and other assets of the business. Basically, these groups of ratios indicate how well the operations of a business are leading to profit-making. The most common types of profitability ratios are return on profit, return on assets, and return on equity.

a. Profit Margin Ratio

The profit margin ratio is also known as the sales ratio or gross profit ratio. This type of profitability ratio measures the amount of net income that

Table 8.4   Sample Balance Sheet: Vertical Format Mr. Adofo and Sons – Balance Sheet for the Year Ended March 31, 2018

	GH₵	GH₵
Non-current assets		
Fixtures and fittings		18,000
Current assets		
Inventory	12,000	
Trade receivables	5,800	
Cash at bank and in hand	2,300	
	20,100	
Current liabilities		
Trade payables	(8,200)	
Net current assets		11,900
Net assets		29,900
Capital		
Cash introduced		25,000
Retained earnings		11,000
		36,000
Add: Net profit for the year		9,400
		45,400
Less: Drawings		(15,500)
		29,900

Table created by authors

accrues to a business with each generated sale (in cedis). It is determined by comparing the business' net income and net sales. The profit margin ratio is computed based on the sole data in the income statement. Higher profit margins indicate better cost control in the business or higher return on every cedi of revenue. Using the income statement prepared for Adofo and Sons in the preceding sections, the profit margin is computed hereafter.

$$\text{Profit margin} = \frac{\text{Net income}\,(\text{Net earnings})}{\text{Sales}\,(\text{Total net revenues})} = \frac{\text{GH₵}\,19,400}{\text{GH₵}\,40,400} = 0.48$$

Therefore, for every GH₵1 in sales, Adofo and Sons as a business generates profits of about 48 pesewas.

b. Return on Assets

The return on assets ratio measures the amount of profit a business makes as a percentage of the value of its total assets. It shows how much income a business has made for every cedi invested in assets. After the computation of the return on assets (ROA), a low return on assets is probably an indication that the business is not using its assets productively. To calculate the return on investment, data from both the income statement and the balance sheet are needed.

$$\text{Return on assets} = \frac{\text{Net income} \left(\text{Net earnings} \right)}{\text{Total assets}} = \frac{\text{GH₵} 19,400}{\text{GH₵ } 129,900} = 0.15$$

The interpretation of the above is that, for every GH₵1 invested in assets by Adofo and Sons, there is a return of around 15 pesewas or profits of around 15 pesewas per cedi. Although the profit percentage of profits differs from industry to industry, generally, the ROA is normally better when it is higher. It is therefore prudent to compare a business's ROA to that of other businesses in the same industry or against its ROA figures from past years.

c. Return on Equity

Return on equity (ROE) is also known as return on investment (ROI). It is of utmost importance to companies because stockholders are always interested in how much money they can gain from their investments. Thus, these stockholders use the return on equity as a key performance indicator. The return on equity is therefore a measure of a business's ability to generate profits from the investment made by shareholders. Better still, return on investment shows how much profit is generated on each cedi of shareholders' investment. The ROE is calculated by dividing the business's net income by the stockholder's equity. Assuming the stockholder's equity to be GH₵150,000, the ROE will then be computed as such:

$$\text{Return on equity} = \frac{\text{Net Income}}{\text{Stockholders' equity}} = \frac{\text{GH₵} 19,400}{\text{GH₵} 150,000} = 0.13 = 13\%$$

From the above, for every cedi invested by the shareholders of Adofo and Sons, the business or company earns around 13% return. It should be noted that debt funding (which is not provided by the owners) might have been obtained to finance some assets of the business. As such, the value of the owner's equity is normally comparatively lower than the total value of the business' assets.

8.3.2 *Liquidity Ratios*

Liquidity ratios are used in measuring a business's ability to pay off current debts without going in for external funding. It compares current assets to current liabilities to determine how fast a business can transform its current assets to pay off debts as they become due. Creditors perceive safety when the liquidity ratios of a business are high. However, very high liquidity ratios may be an indication that the business is not effectively using its current assets. Examples of liquidity ratios are current ratios and quick ratios.

a. Current Ratio

The current ratio evaluates the capacity of a business to handle its short-term liability in terms of payment with its current assets. When the current ratio is greater than 1.0, then the business can be considered to be well-positioned to pay its current or short-term liabilities as they fall due. The current ratio shows the proportion of a business's current assets to its current liabilities. It is calculated by dividing current assets over current liabilities as depicted below.

$$\text{Current ratio} = \frac{\text{Current assets}}{\text{Current liabilities}} = \frac{\text{GH}\cancel{C}\,20,100}{\text{GH}\cancel{C}\,8,200} = 2.45$$

From the above, it can be deduced that Adofo and Sons have enough current assets to pay off 245 per cent (2.45*100) of its current liabilities. The business is highly leveraged and vastly risky.

b. Quick Ratio

The quick ratio, also known as the acidity test, is a liquidity ratio that is used to measure the ability of a business to rely only on quick assets to pay off current liabilities as they fall due. It evaluates the extent to which a business can sort its current liabilities without having to rely on selling inventory.

This type of ratio is considered as being more stringent as it eliminates inventory (the least liquid current asset). The quick ratio is calculated below.

$$\text{Quick ratio} = \frac{\text{Current Assets} - \text{Inventory}}{\text{Current liabilities}} = \frac{\text{GH}\cancel{C}\,20,100 - 12,000}{\text{GH}\cancel{C}\,8,200} = 0.99$$

The interpretation of this is that Adofo and Sons can easily pay off its current assets by 99% (0.99*100) using its quick assets.

8.3.3 Debt Utilisation Ratios

Debt utilisation ratios present a complete picture of a business's financial health or its solvency. It indicates the percentage of the business' assets that have been provided by debt funding. The use of debt funding is riskier than equity funding since the business is obligated to pay these debts irrespective of whether it makes a profit or not. Also, unanticipated negative occurrences in the business environment such as recession, to a larger extent have negative implications on indebted businesses than those that rely more on owner's equity. Debt-to-real asset ratio and time interest earned ratio are examples of debt utilisation ratios.

a. Debt-to-Real Asset Ratio

The debt-to-real asset ratio is also termed the total debt to total assets ratio. It is a leverage ratio that describes the total amount of debt of a business, compared to assets. This metric allows a cross-industry analysis or comparison of leverage. In this context, the higher the ratio is, then the higher the extent of leverage and therefore the financial risk. To compute the debt-to-real asset ratio, the following equation is used.

$$\text{Debt to total assets} = \frac{\text{Debt}\,(\text{Total liabilities})}{\text{Total assets}} = \frac{\text{GH}\cancel{C}\,8,200}{\text{GH}\cancel{C}\,29,900} = 0.27$$

Hence, for every GH₵1 of Adofo and Sons' total assets, 27 per cent (0.27*100) is financed through debt funding whilst the remaining 63 per cent is financed through owner's equity.

b. Time Interest Earned Ratio

Time interest ratio indicates the financial standing of a business to pay off interest charged by creditors, considering its current assets. A low time interest earned ratio communicates that a little decrease in earnings can push the business into financial straits. The time interest earned ratio is calculated by dividing the earnings before interest and tax (EBIT) by the interest charged. So, assuming Adofo and Sons had an EBIT of GH₵560 and interest of GH₵40, the time interest earned ratio will be computed as:

$$\text{Time interest earned} = \frac{\text{Earnings before interest and tax}\,(\text{EBIT})}{\text{Interest}} = \frac{\text{GH₵}\,560}{\text{GH₵}\,40} = 14$$

The above means that Adofo and Sons can bear an interest of 14 times more than its current interest expense.

8.3.4 Asset Utilisation Ratios

Asset utilisation ratios are used for calculating the total revenue a business earns for every cedi of an asset it owns. A higher asset utilisation means that the business is operating efficiently with each cedi of the asset it has. As such, a business that uses its assets productively will have higher rates of returns on assets as compared to lesser efficient competitors. Managers can also rely on asset utilisation ratios to determine the area(s) of inefficiency in their production. In short, asset utilisation ratios are normally used to compare the efficiency of a business over time. Three types of asset utilisation ratios are discussed in this section; receivables turnover, inventory turnover, and total asset turnover.

a. Receivable Turnover Ratio

The asset turnover ratio shows the number of times a business collects its account receivable in a given accounting year. It avers how the business is quickly able to issue credits to customers as well as amass payments for goods sold on credit. A high turnover ratio designates an amalgamation of a conservative credit policy and an aggressive collections department, as well as a number of high-quality customers. On the flip side, a low turnover ratio denotes a chance to collect excessively old accounts receivable that are needlessly tethering working capital. A business' inability to collect these funds also means it cannot make profits. The receivable turnover ratio is computed by dividing sales over accounts receivable.

$$\text{Receivables turnover} = \frac{\text{Sales}\,(\text{Total net revenue})}{\text{Receivables}} = \frac{\text{GH₵}\,40,000}{\text{GH₵}\,5,800} = 6.70$$

From above, Adofo and Sons collected its accounts receivable 6.70 times in the accounting year in view.

b. Inventory Turnover Ratio

The inventory turnover ratio measures the number of times a business sells and replaces its inventory within an accounting year. A high inventory turnover ratio may mean that the business has greater efficiency. However, it may also negatively suggest a possibility of lost sales as a result of insufficient inventory. It is computed by dividing the business' sales over the inventory as indicated below.

$$\text{Inventory turnover} = \frac{\text{Sales}(\text{Total net revenue})}{\text{Inventory}} = \frac{\text{GH}\cancel{C}\,40,000}{\text{GH}\cancel{C}\,12,000} = 3.33$$

The figure obtained means that in the accounting year or period, Adofo and Sons replaced inventory 3.33 times.

c. Total Asset Turnover Ratio

The total asset turnover ratio measures a business' capability to use all of its assets to generate sales by matching net sales with average total assets. Better still, the total asset turnover ratio demonstrates how a business uses its assets to generate sales. It proves that a business is using its assets productively. Computing the total asset turnover entails dividing the business' sales over total assets.

$$\text{Total asset turnover} = \frac{\text{Sales}(\text{Total net revenue})}{\text{Total assets}} = \frac{\cancel{C}\,40,000}{\cancel{C}\,29,900} = 1.34$$

In the example above, Adofo and Sons earned GH₵1.34 for each cedi of assets held by the business.

8.4 Conclusion

Understanding financial statements and its implication for investment and the overall success of any business venture cannot be underestimated. Investors who expect their investment to yield good returns are always keen on reading and interpreting financial statements and ratios to guide their business decisions. Likewise, in business, shareholders require accountability in order to ensure their investments are in safe hands and are being used judiciously to achieve intended objectives. It also underscores the critical nature of financial information in business management, while making it necessary for businesses to keep proper books of record on how funds have been applied.

In the post-COVID-19 period, it has become more important for businesses to provide real time information to the shareholders. Businesses should therefore engage the services of professionals to prepare simple accounting software for them to manage their financial records. These simple accounting software for small and medium enterprises will enable them to identify the driving factors for their costs and revenue enhancing factors. If costs are minimised and revenue maximised, the businesses will make profits and satisfy their shareholders.

Businesses should also engage the services of professionals to prepare their annual accounts and file their tax returns for them. Timely submission of financial statements to shareholders and filing of accounts and tax returns will make the businesses good corporate entities. Being a good corporate entity helps attract and retain both employees and customers. In the period of the post-COVID-19 pandemic, organisations need to ensure a high retention of their employees and customers to be able to bounce back to normalcy after the shock and the negative effect of the onset of the pandemic.

References

Abad-Segura, E. & González-Zamar, M.D. (2020). Research analysis on emerging technologies in corporate accounting. *Mathematics*, 8(9), 1589.

Abrohms, S. & Schuler, K. (2019). A balance sheet analysis of the CFA franc zone. *Studies in Applied Economics*, 143, 15–20

Agyemang, G., O'Dwyer, B. & Unerman, J. (2019). NGO accountability: Retrospective and prospective academic contributions. *Accounting, Auditing and Accountability Journal*, 32(8), 2353–2366.

Alabdullah, T.T. & Maryanti, E. (2021). Internal control mechanisms in accounting, management, and economy: A review of the literature and suggestions of new investigations. *International Journal of Business and Management Invention*, 10(9), 8–12.

Alawamleh, H.A., Alshibly, M.H.A.A., Tommalieh, A.F.A., Al-Qaryouti, M.Q.H. & Ali, B.J. (2021). The challenges, barriers and advantages of management information system development: Comprehensive review. *Academy of Strategic Management Journal*, 20(5), 1–8.

Al-Hashimy, H.N.H. (2022). A review of accounting manipulation and detection: Technique and prevention methods. *International Journal of Business and Management Invention*, 11(10), 82–89.

Appiah-Konadu, P., Apetorgbor, V.K. & Atanya, O. (2022). Non-financial reporting regulation and the state of sustainability disclosure among banks in sub-Saharan Africa (SSA): A literature review on banks in Ghana and Nigeria. In Ogunyemi, K., Atanya, O., Burgal, V. (eds) *Management and Leadership for a Sustainable Africa, Volume 2: Roles, Responsibilities, and Prospects* (pp. 55–72). Palgrave Macmillan, Cham.

Deno, C.F. (2019). The accounting professional of tomorrow. *The CPA Journal*, 89(9), 14–15.

Edwards, J.R. (2013). *A History of Financial Accounting (RLE Accounting)*. Routledge.

El-Ebiary, Y.A.B., Hatamleh, A., Al Moaiad, Y., Amayreh, K.T., Mohamed, R.R., Al-Haithami, W.A. & Saany, S.I.A. (2023). A review of the effectiveness of management information system in decision making. *Journal of Pharmaceutical Negative Results*, 14(2), 1281–1288.

Elliott, B. & Elliott, J. (2007). *Financial Accounting and Reporting*. Pearson Education.

Geng, X. & Kalargiros, M. (2022). Why does affect matter in accounting: A review of experimental studies on the effect of affect. *Journal of Accounting Literature*, 44(1), 1–39.

Habib, A., Costa, M.D., Huang, H.J., Bhuiyan, M.B.U. & Sun, L. (2020). Determinants and consequences of financial distress: Review of the empirical literature. *Accounting and Finance*, 60(S1), 1023–1075.

Hassan, O.A. & Marston, C. (2019). Corporate financial disclosure measurement in the empirical accounting literature: A review article. *The International Journal of Accounting*, 54(2), 1950006.

Hin, L.H. (2019). Critical review: Future of block chain economy in financial services. *Global Journal of Management and Business Research*, 19(B7), 9–15.

Imhanzenobe, J. (2022). Value relevance and changes in accounting standards: A review of the IFRS adoption literature. *Cogent Business and Management*, 9(1), 2039057.

Jackson, A.B. (2022). Financial statement analysis: A review and current issues. *China Finance Review International*, 12(1), 1–19.

Jiang, S. (2022). September. A survey of research on the effect of tangible assets on capital structure. In *Proceedings of the 2022 International Conference on Business and Policy Studies* (pp. 668–676). Springer Nature Singapore.

Libby, R., Libby, P.A., Short, D.G., Kanaan, G. & Gowing, M. (2004). *Financial Accounting*. McGraw-Hill/Irwin.

Maddox, D. (2022). Accounting's problematic relationship to legitimacy: A review of the critical literature. *Hatfield Graduate Journal of Public Affairs*, 6(1), Article 8. https://doi.org/10.15760/hgjpa.2021.6.7.

Maru, P.K.R. (2022). Emerging trends in accounting standards. Reimagining business education and industry in 2030, 101–114.

Mert, I. (2022). Assessment of accounting evaluation practices: A research-based review of Turkey and Romania. *Contributions to Finance and Accounting* (pp. 62–71). Springer Cham, Australia.

Munna, A. (2021). Business model: Literature review. *PINISI Discretion Review*, 4(2), 1–6.

O'Connell, M. & Ward, A.M. (2020). Shareholder theory/shareholder value. In: Idowu, S., Schmidpeter, R., Capaldi, N., Zu, L., Del Baldo, M., Abreu, R. (eds) *Encyclopedia of Sustainable Management* (pp. 1–7). Springer Cham, Switzerland.

Pelz, M. (2019). Can management accounting be helpful for young and small companies? Systematic review of a paradox. *International Journal of Management Reviews*, 21(2), 256–274.

Ranatarisza, M.M., Rahayu, S.M., Hanum, L. & Ari, D.P.S. (2022). The intention to use accounting software on SMES for becoming bankable company. *International Journal of Organizational Behavior and Policy*, 1(1), 15–26.

Rodríguez-Fernández, M., Gaspar-González, A.I. & Sánchez-Teba, E.M. (2020). Sustainable social responsibility through stakeholders engagement. *Corporate Social Responsibility and Environmental Management*, 27(6), 2425–2436.

Rogosic, A. (2019). Accounting outsourcing issues. *Eurasian Journal of Business and Management*, 7(3), 44–53.

Roychowdhury, S., Shroff, N. & Verdi, R.S. (2019). The effects of financial reporting and disclosure on corporate investment: A review. *Journal of Accounting and Economics*, 68(2–3), 101246.

Sanad, Z. & Al-Sartawi, A. (2021). Financial statements fraud and data mining: A review. In: Musleh Al-Sartawi, A.M., Razzaque, A., Kamal, M.M. (eds) *Artificial Intelligence Systems and the Internet of Things in the Digital Era: Proceedings of EAMMIS 2021* (pp. 407–414), Springer, Cham.

Shahrina, K., Meem, S.S., Sarker, D., Hossain, R. & Amin, M.A. (2022). A comprehensive review and analysis on decentralized payment gateways. In: Association for Computing Machinery, *Proceedings of the 2nd International Conference on Computing Advancements* (pp. 359–366).

Stauffer, M.T. & Takahashi, T.T. (2023). A history and commentary on thrust/drag bookkeeping. *AIAA SCITECH 2023 Forum* (1553).

Stojković, M. & Jeremijev, V. (2021). Price formation in trade companies. *International Review*, 3–4, 66–70.

Sundaram, R., Sharma, D. & Shakya, D. (2020). Digital transformation of business models: A systematic review of impact on revenue and supply chain. *International Journal of Management*, 11(5), 9–21.

Tawiah, V. (2019). The state of IFRS in Africa. *Journal of Financial Reporting and Accounting*, 17(4), 635–649.

Topor, D.I., Akram, U., Fülop, M.T., Căpușneanu, S. & Ionescu, C.A. (2021). E-accounting: Future challenges and perspectives. *CSR and Management Accounting Challenges in a Time of Global Crises*, 18 (1), 35–52.

Wolf, T., Kuttner, M., Feldbauer-Durstmüller, B. & Mitter, C. (2020). What we know about management accountants' changing identities and roles–a systematic literature review. *Journal of Accounting and Organizational Change*, 16(3), 311–347.

Case Study

Case Material – Financial and Management Accounting

Douglas and Pamela Frank are a married couple. They both worked for a railroad company for 30 years. At age 57, Douglas and age 52, Pamela retired and moved to the small town of Ovilla, TX, which has a population of approximately 3,500 residents. When the Franks moved to the town, they decided to start a childcare business in their home called Nanna's House.

Nanna's House is licensed by the state. The state charges an annual fee of $225 to maintain the license. Insurance is required at a cost of $3,840 annually. The facility is licensed to care for a maximum of six children. The Franks charge a fee of $800 per month for each child. The monthly fee is based on a full day of care, from 8:00 a.m. to 4:00 p.m. If additional time is required beyond 4:00 p.m., parents must pay an additional charge of $15 per hour for each child. The couple provides two meals and a snack for the children. The cost of the meals and snacks is $3.20 per child per day. There are six children currently enrolled.

The facility is very nice. It is an 820-square-foot addition to their home that was built in 1964. The Franks purchased the home and completed the renovations for $79,500, and they believe the addition has a useful life of 25 years. The facility has a large open space for play, reading, and other activities. There is a section for sleeping which contains small cots. The facility is equipped with a small kitchen, two bathrooms, and a small laundry area. The day-care increased the Franks' utility cost by $50 each month.

During the first week of operations, the washer and dryer stopped working. Both appliances were old and had been used by the couple for many years. The old appliances cost a total of $440. While a laundry room was not initially a necessity, it became increasingly important for laundering the soiled clothes of the children, blankets, and sheets. A company nearby, Red Oak Laundry and Dry Cleaning, can launder clothing for the Franks, including pick-up and delivery, for $52 per month.

Alternatively, the Franks can take clothes to the laundromat once a week, which is three miles away (one way). The applicable mileage rate is $0.56/

mile. They can launder the clothes themselves at a cost of $8 per week. The self-service alternative does not include detergent or fabric sheets. The couple would need to purchase these items in order to use the laundromat. Purchasing laundry supplies in bulk from Mega Mart would cost $35 every quarter. The final alternative is for the Franks to purchase a washer and dryer. The cost of the appliances is: washer $420 and dryer $380. The additional accessories for both appliances, needed for installation, cost $43.72. The store will deliver the appliances at a total cost of $35. The cost of installing the appliances is free. Both appliances are expected to last 8 years. According to the manufacturer, the washer will increase energy costs by $120 per year. The dryer will increase energy costs by $145 per year.

The Franks need some assistance in decision-making and evaluation. They have contacted Emily Smith, their accountant, to provide some advice.

Requirements

Respond to the following Case Discussion Questions to help Douglas and Pamela make their decisions.

Case Discussion Questions

(If necessary, the Franks will use straight line depreciation. For monthly calculations, use 4.33 weeks per month.)

1. Consider the different types of costs discussed in this course. List the costs discussed in the case and provide one specific example of each.

2. Based on the information provided, what information is relevant to the decision to purchase the appliances? What information is irrelevant to the decision to purchase the appliances? Why?

3. What could it cost the couple to launder clothes? Show your detailed calculations for each.

4. The couple has made a significant investment in this business. How long will it take for the couple to recoup their investment? Is the time required to recoup the investment a good measure of the success of the company? If not, how would you measure the success of the company? Explain.

5. As Emily Smith, prepare a letter to the Franks advising them on their laundry needs. What is your recommendation and why?

6. The Franks have a wait list for their day-care. They can hire an employee for $9 per hour for 40 hours each week. With the additional employee, the Franks can accept three additional children.

   Should the Franks hire the additional employee? Show your detailed calculations.

7. The Franks' home can accommodate a maximum of nine children. They can move the day-care from their home to a rented space in town, which can accommodate up to 14 children. The space will cost $650 per month and the utilities will cost $125 per month. Additionally, insurance will now cost the Franks $5,000 per year. Per state regulations, each adult can supervise no more than three children. As Emily Smith, prepare a letter to the Franks advising them on their space options. Should they continue to operate the facility at home or should they rent space in town?

   How many children should they accept? How many employees will they need to hire? Show your detailed calculations for each scenario.

Source: http://www.na-businesspress.com/JAF/GatesS_Web15_7_.pdf

Index

Printed in the United States
by Baker & Taylor Publisher Services

Printed in the United States
by Baker & Taylor Publisher Services